Praise for Jill Butler's *Create the Space You Deserve*

"Jill Butler brings character, clarity, and creativity to the art of making a home. Both visionary and catalytic, she sparks and inspires her reader. In her hands, the making of a home is a spiritual practice."

  —JULIA CAMERON, author of *The Artist's Way*

"Jill's creative energy was expressed on many articles that graced the tables at Sur La Table and later the tables of our customers. Now with Jill's new book we will all share the simple steps to recreating the spaces around us. Her clean, crisp approach to design and use of color comes through on every page. Let Jill inspire you to look at your personal spaces with a new eye. This book makes an easy transition from old to new. I felt like I could do some of these creative changes with the things I had available in my home already. You will love every page."

  —RENEE BEHNKE, President Emeritus and owner of
  Sur La Table kitchen stores

"Though I've always believed in Jill's principle of 'the artistic journey to expressing yourself through your home,' her new book unclutters that journey with wonderful, inspiring signposts and goals that give each of us permission, no matter our age or circumstance, to create a nest that is unique, reaffirming, and truly deserving of who we are and what we might become! Could be she has convinced me I am finally ready to build that shack in the woods I've wanted all my life!"

  —MARY RANDOLPH CARTER, author of *For the Love of Old*

"Jill Butler has a way of leading the reader right on through the emotions of the design process without pulling any punches while showing how important our houses are to self-image. There's a lot here for architects and designers to use and to keep in mind."

  —MICHAEL J. CROSBIE, author, architect, critic, and head of the
  Department of Architecture at the University of Hartford

"Create the Space You Deserve is a self portrait of an artist's personal evolution through the reconstruction of her home. As coaches, it's impressive to see how Jill utilizes her education to create a profile of her journey from one transition to another in full creative and artistic expression. She has a lot to reveal and will keep the reader thoroughly entertained."

  —JOE RUBIN/MONICA LANDRY, Vocalfit Solutions®

create the space
you deserve

JILL BUTLER

photographs by Lisa Bousquet

*an artistic
journey
to expressing
yourself
through your
home*

skirt!®

GUILFORD, CONNECTICUT
AN IMPRINT OF THE GLOBE PEQUOT PRESS

To buy books in quantity for corporate use or incentives,
call **(800) 962-0973 or e-mail premiums@GlobePequot.com.**

skirt!® is an attitude . . . spirited, independent, outspoken, serious,
playful and irreverent, sometimes controversial, always passionate.

skirt! is an imprint of The Globe Pequot Press.
skirt!® is a registered trademark of Morris Publishing Group, LLC,
and is used with express permission.

Cover and text design by Nancy Freeborn
Photography by Lisa Bousquet
All text, illustrations and collages by Jill Butler

Library of Congress Cataloging-in-Publication Data
Butler, Jill.
   Create the space you deserve : an artistic journey to expressing
yourself through your home / Jill Butler.
      p. cm.
   ISBN 978-1-59921-290-6
  1. Interior decoration. I. Title.
   NK2115.B925 2008
   747—dc22

                              2008003799

Printed in the United States of America
10 9 8 7 6 5 4 3 2

I dedicate this book to my brother, York, the now Bro' Angel. I am listening loud.

For many years, I have "shown up on the page" for my personal growth. And today I acknowledge and dedicate this book to the two people who have guided, coached, and encouraged me from the highest level of integrity one could be fortunate to know and experience. Thank you from every fiber of my being, Joe Rubin and Monica Landry.

I further dedicate this book to my spiritual sisters: Karen Beckwith, Maureen Benun, Elise Kroll, Elsa Nelson, and Daya Soudan who have stood with me in tears and in hilarity. I am grateful to be in sisterhood with you beautiful, creative "wonder-women."

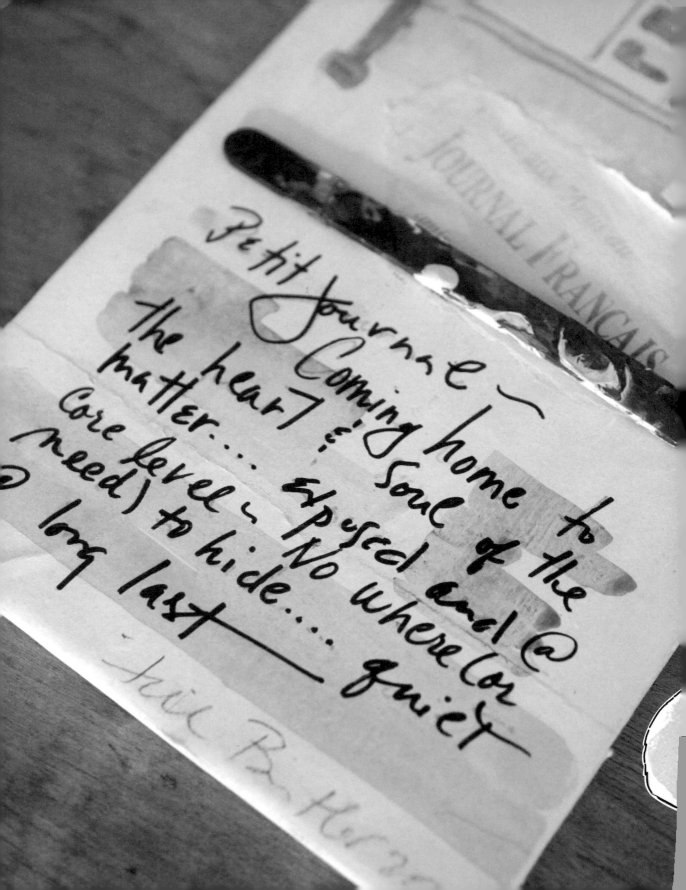

contents

introduction: why bother?

When you plan a trip, you make reservations, figure out an itinerary, fill up the gas tank, and take along the appropriate maps. And, because life is like that, there will be detours and serendipity along the way.

Whatever brought you to the point of wanting to make changes in your living environment is personal to you. Remembering that this, too, is a journey will make it more fun and beneficial. Upon arrival, you can look back and acknowledge your adventure and achievement of having created a new space, home, or apartment that feels unique to you and answers the call to support and nurture your needs.

This journey takes planning and work. So that part of you that wants it all magically handed to you, I understand, but I can also say it's far more powerful when you personally invest in yourself and your project. And when you think of this not as work, but as play, everything changes.

1

why bother?

exactly, why bother?

move on . . . don't move on

change . . . don't change

take responsibility . . . i'd rather not

decide . . . let someone else

bother . . . don't bother

life changes are like this
back and forth, back and forth

creating a space or a home
for oneself . . .
that's another volleyball game

it's too hard
i don't know how
what if . . .
i don't have the money,
energy, or time

negative self-talk
can excuse us every time
from creating
what we want

trust me

i waffled
i whined
i wavered

then i got positive . . . negative
fired up and cooled down
as quickly as i got courageous
i got scared

gradually
with time

help from friends
the goddess above
my coach and
my longing for change
i decided!
and
what i decided was –
i was worth the effort and
i deserved the best
i could create
for myself

Life Changes: Creating a New Space

So one life ends . . . through divorce in my case. Another one is about to begin—this one, single. It's the filling between the slices of the beginning and the end that interests me. Ready-made is not my style. The heart and soul of this middle, this process of getting from beginning to end, is what keeps me interested in life. I like the adventure. The unfolding story. I love the process. I won't pretend that it's always easy, but that's part of the journey. You'll see as we go along. I'm not thirty, I'm a bunch more than that. So this is not a young chick story; this is a life-lived story. It is, however, a story for all ages. It's about hope, essentially.

*looking back
to go forward*

Don't Just Settle

Settling for just any roof over my head was not a choice. No matter what people have said about us, or how unworthy we may feel at the moment, or how difficult it may be to say what we want, we deserve the very best we can create for ourselves. I know this situation intimately. I have been here more than once. I have now heard from countless women who have made the effort to create a difference in their lives.

The Space Between
the Beginning and the End

In the nick of time, I found my love house, bought it, and closed on it. I had five days in which to move. I chose to camp in the now "guest nest" of my new house and to move everything all at once. The moving van arrived on June 5th. Air France (my soon-to-be-divorced husband) was landing in the U.S. on June 6th, and the tour boat of his invited guests was arriving on June 10th.

3

this . . .

Between the beginning and the end is the unfolding story. This is a step-by-step process so that you, too, can lose your mind and open your heart to creating exactly what you want for yourself in your living space, even when those around you are scratching their heads and wondering what you're up to.

. . . is that.

new steps

In speaking with other women, I discovered that there are many of us who have used this process of creating our nest as a stepping stone into our new life. Investing emotionally in our personal living space resembles something like this: "I felt afraid. I felt lousy about myself and life in general. Taking the first steps to making changes felt like walking for the first time after having been cut wide open. I noticed I felt even worse when I saw myself not taking steps. So I started doing the best I could. Eventually, the process took over."

Any sort of life transition can spark the need or desire for a new living space.

There are a myriad of scenarios.

I'm graduated. I'm an adult,
I'm getting a job, I hope.
I have to live somewhere, somehow.
This can be an ouch!

I'm in an abusive relationship,
plain and simple, I need to move.
A wake-up call

My life partner has died and I'm
longing to nurture the next me.
A punch

The town where I live has ceased to
harmonize with me.
A pinch

About thirty houses into my search . . . I found it. The house was in an exclusive neighborhood and stuck out like a sore thumb. The brush in the front yard was up to my knees. Fallen trees were everywhere. Upon entering the house, I discovered it had good bones. "This house just needs to be loved," was my immediate reaction. Most of the work was aesthetic, not mechanical. It was my therapy as I worked through a life-threatening illness. I would putter, paint, and design every weekend. Through careful editing and constant vigilance that "less is more," I created the peace I need at this station in life. Never would I have thought it possible to own my dream home. My home became an expression of my soul.

SUSAN, 48
FINANCIAL ADVISOR
KILLINGWORTH, CT

My home is way too big,
and it's time to do something about it.

A shift

Our special first home needs to expand to
accommodate our expanding family.

A celebration

I'm tired of paying rent and losing equity.
I'm ready to be an owner.

A milestone

Wherever we are in our life experience,
we're creating that experience
   —even when we feel broke or broken.
We can move the molecules
   —they're moving anyway,
so we might as well have some say
about where they're going.

*Think of fear
as excitement . . .
this helps
   a lot!*

Serenity and peace
were my vision for
my home. I knew
I wanted to be
surrounded by life,
plants, and flowers.
I wanted a place to
retreat from the
world and to feel
at peace with life.

MICHELLE, 34
LOAN SUPERVISOR
LENEXA, KS

Emotionally
wounded
or launched
into the
world—
they can
feel the
same.

so, why bother?

The difference between when we just do "whatever" versus actually allowing ourselves to feel our feelings and acknowledge our needs is in the great rewards we experience. Throwing ourselves against a wall and hoping for a positive result is not usually successful. There's a difference between knowing what you need, sometimes letting those around you help, and blowing in the wind, wishing, wanting, and hoping for a white knight.

The conscious journey is worth the effort and eventually is cause for celebration.

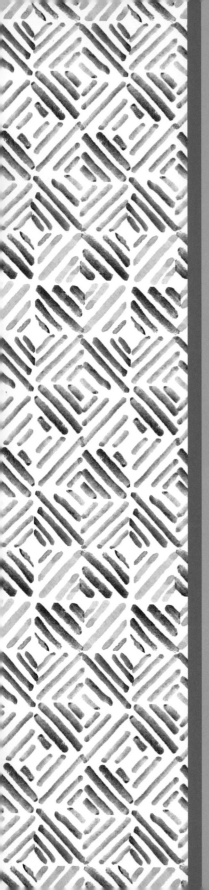

clearing
    the crud
quiets
    the mind

1

clearing the crud

I **don't know why this is so hard,** but it is—in this moment the garbage bags get filled, the Dumpster waits at the back door, the date is set. Something new is about to happen in your life, because you've literally decided to clear the way for the new. Trust me, this is true!

It's simply more work to live with clutter—more than you'll ever want or need. The stuff literally drags down our energy and makes us feel bad about it—and ourselves!

At age ten, my father cured me of accumulating. One day, in our basement, I discovered that all of my "stored" stuff had been ditched. I cried for days. The fact that he didn't discuss it with me made a strong impression. In the end, I didn't actually miss anything, which taught me a lifetime lesson. But I still don't know how I feel about not having been consulted.

9

Hopefully, this moment will arise no matter the reason—the "clearing the crud" moment. As always, you have choices. You can either set a deadline or deal with it well in advance of your move.

Of course, your other alternative is to:

- Worry about doing it and let it continue to wear you down.
- Wait till the last moment, when the moving van is pulling in the drive.
- Move it all, paying by the pound, or hauling it with the kindness of good friends (hopefully, they still are).
- Pay for a storage unit.
- Move it all into the new house . . . and panic over all the boxes that might never get unpacked.
- Try to cram it all into the new space . . . not very inviting—even claustrophobic.
- Finally, get totally depressed and angry at yourself for not clearing the crud early in the game.

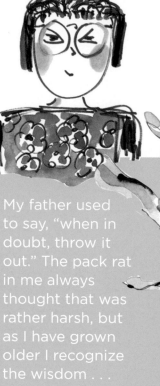

My father used to say, "when in doubt, throw it out." The pack rat in me always thought that was rather harsh, but as I have grown older I recognize the wisdom . . . easier said than done. I'm still thinking about all those boxes in the basement that have stayed unopened all these years. Getting rid of the old will create room for the new . . . or just create more space. I can definitely use more of that!

ELISE, 52
DIRECTOR OF SALES,
WRITER
SAN FRANCISCO, CA

"The Store-All Housing Development"

One of America's hot new trends is storage units.

"We build units for our crud which we seem to value more than the homeless for whom we build virtually nothing."

—Lynne Twist, author of *The Soul of Money*

For a long time, I had been uncomfortable in my home. It was messy and full of unnecessary things and clutter. I travel a great deal, and when I get home I am tired. I had allowed my space to become so messy that I was uncomfortable in it and ashamed to have anyone come into it. Something radical had to happen! My goal was to feel peace, order, and harmony in my home. And the one major thing I wish I had known when I started to change my ways and to clean up was how easy and joyful the process was going to be. For me, it was an attitude change and a desire of the heart.

JUDITH, 63
SONOMA, CA

11

Lightening the Load

I worked at home in the barn for years, and I had hundreds of projects complete and incomplete—or in process—files from clients that had lingered, photos left uncatalogued, old computer manuals, long-ago dismissed drawings, collage materials yellowing beyond use.
You get the idea.

It was time to cut to the chase, which for me means get moving, get honest, get relentless. For six months, one hour a day, I gave myself to cleansing this part of my life.

Every day I got lighter and felt better.

I gave every item the once-over:

 Does this fit?

    Is this who I am today?

        Is this object slowing me down with guilt?

Is this treasure from my aunt really
my statement of me or her?

    Is this purple hat the one
I want to garden in?

Does this chair comfort me?

    Is this funky footstool
a keeper?

It makes me smile, so the answer is

yes.

Having successfully spent one hour a day, as decided, I managed to create fresh files for needed papers, sort the giveaway piles, and celebrate the huge black garbage bags (somebody needs to design designer garbage bags) that went out, if not nightly, often, leaving no temptation of going back in.

A friend taught me the tricolor sticker method of marking everything:

● RED (dump)

● YELLOW (sell)

● BLUE (keep)

I vowed not to spend hours, days, or weeks trying to place my near-homeless items with those who might be able to take them off my hands. I also vowed not to fill the landfill, and I wasn't of the mind to create posters, hang them, advertise, and get helpers to drag everything outside, nor to price, tag, and sit around waiting for folks to find me.

- I didn't have a move date.
- I hadn't yet sold the barn where I lived.
- I hadn't bought a new house, but I *was* looking, and I had my vision of my new life in my mind's eye.
- The only thing I knew for sure was that I needed to get started on clearing the crud.

Antique Treasures and Family Heirlooms

While it's easy to toss the piles of meaningless junk that have accumulated over the years, it's much more emotionally challenging to make decisions about objects that have sentimental value. Often, making the hard decisions is painful and guilt-producing. You'll experience enormous relief if you're willing to make honest decisions about how you feel about these things.

Choose the one thing that really resonates with you and grounds the memory of that family member, letting the rest of it go. It will bring you a certain measure of comfort if you find homes for the things you're ready to release, or if you find a considerate dealer.

I answered one simple question: What is the intention for this space? (The space was the room over the double garage.) I moved the two twenty-gallon trash bins directly under the upstairs windows and screamed for joy as the stuff flew out the window. I celebrated the purge with a decorating trip with a friend, a bottle of wine, and big hugs from my husband, and I found space that serves us all: Office for two, overnight guests, and recovered pride in showing off the space.

Whew!

LISA, 46
GYM OWNER
EAST HADDAM, CT

get those trash bins and go at it!

The No-Tag Tag Sale

I decided not to waste precious time tagging and pricing all of the items for my sale. So, I invented the no-tag tag sale—my best idea ever! Once the barn was empty and 95 percent of the furniture was moved out, I asked five to six groups of related friends to drop by at a time convenient for them. For example, the gals from the bank came after closing hours on a Wednesday evening, my office-building-mates came for drinks at 6:00 p.m. on another night, and the young mother group organized by a friend came at 10:00 a.m. one morning.

Here's what I did—this is just my own weird way, you'll invent your own!

1. Put it all out.

2. Use the floor for displays, and group items by category: table stuff, cooking stuff, furniture, and nameless treasures.

3. Price nothing—no tags, no stickers.

When each group arrived, I made this announcement:

"Here's the deal: My goal is to have everything go home with someone this week. There are no prices marked. Make your pile of what you can't live without, and together we'll figure out the price . . .

16

and I promise you, you'll go home with what you want!" It was important to remember that everything was leaving, going home to a new home . . . not mine.

Now, for larger items, you can name a price, even if it's a high number. As incentive, include something for free or practically free. Remember the goal: It's all going, and they are the ones

carrying it out . . . no promises of deliveries. In this hilarious way, the displays dwindled. I made some money—who knows, maybe more or less than a real tag sale, but certainly less painful. At the end of two and a half weeks, I had sold everything except some remnants that I donated to a tag sale benefiting candidates running for local office. Nothing went to the landfill, and nothing was trashed! Plus, it was fun!

When complete, **CELEBRATE**—and don't be so quick to fill it up again! Live with the empty spaces—you might even get used to them.

Give yourself time to thoughtfully decide what you might want new. When it's clear, go find it. Do not deny yourself.

drawing from
all sides
of my brain

creating a
written picture

DARE TO ASK FOR WHAT YOU WANT

Now that you've said goodbye to the physical crud, here's a chance for a different kind of clearing . . . the emotional.

See what comes, or goes, when you fool around with a paintbrush, track your dreams, or listen to what you're saying. Seeing where you are will help you see where you're headed. Releasing the old makes room for new opportunities, and a new vision for your life and your space!

Some of us love words. Others love visuals. Some of us love both. When launching a new house project, I usually start writing first, unless I find a visual that's exactly what I want. Writing it out reminds me of what I'm thinking and gives me a place to add, edit, and change my mind. Tear sheets from magazines, pictures from books, or photographs help hold the image in the mind's eye.

19

A Healing House
transforms as we do

Creating a soulful space, or a nest, is not a new idea for women. What might be new is creating the nest that supports *you* and makes *you* feel loved and nurtured when your world might not. In these moments, it's not easy to nurture ourselves; our self-esteem may be bashed, beaten, and wobbly.

Taking the time to understand the deeper need—taking the time to understand what we want, need, or are thinking about for a new space, home, living situation—is the FIRST STEP.

Choices!
Choosing what we want and need versus just settling, reacting, accepting.

Listening and Hearing
what we are saying

We women love to talk; it's a huge part of our process. It's how we share with each other. Sometimes when we're overwhelmed and confused in the midst of change, by actually *hearing* what we're saying when we talk out loud, and *listening to ourselves,* we begin to understand what we're thinking and feeling.

Other times, it's simply a repeat of the same old, same old. A good friend might mention that she's already heard this story many times. It's more likely whining, no longer useful, and time to move on.

Good Morning Writing
another way of talking, hearing, and seeing how we feel

Writing out the anger, frustration, stagnation, feelings of hopelessness, and despair that most often accompany our waking clears the way for a better day. This writing process, known as "morning pages," was created by Julia Cameron in her 1992 classic *The Artist's Way.* Please note that this book and process are not exclusively for artists.

It's time to speak up and say what you want. Sometimes we don't know. Sometimes we're just afraid to say it out loud.

It's for all of us who want to experience life differently. As Cameron suggests, and I have found to be true, three pages of writing every morning can make a huge difference in your outlook and life circumstances. After a page and a half of venting, the tone will gradually change and hope will begin to creep in, along with new ideas.

Capturing Dreams That Have Captured Us
dreams give us deep and powerful messages

I had a dream. . . . I am in prison. My husband is my jailer. He is pacing back and forth in front of my cell. Hands clenched on the bars, desperate, I am watching him. Back and forth, back and forth he goes.

I see favorite paintings of my creation hanging on the stone wall across the room, where he is pacing. They are hanging crudely from huge, rusted nails. I cannot get to

chained to the prison wall my work, my art my creativity

Escaping the prison as a butterfly

them. My heart is pounding. How am I ever to get free?

In my dream I must have thrown up a prayer, because I suddenly see a clear answer to the question.

Turn yourself into a butterfly and go out on his shoulder . . . he will never know.

and i flew out on the shoulder of my sailer

This dream and this butterfly have remained with me. It's one of those dreams that I'll never forget. It is why I often refer to my cottage as the butterfly house. Pay attention and be open to what your dreams might have to say.

a fat paintbrush

has a lot to say

I'm not sure how this process first started, but I once found myself seated in the breakfast nook in my bathrobe with my morning coffee, writing bold words with a fat paintbrush on recycled Xerox paper. This was not art . . . it was simple expression.

Without thinking, the paintbrush took off dabbing and slapping the paint across the page. Thoughts were being pulled out of me—thoughts that felt hopeful, soulful, and ridiculously impossible. This process became a way of expressing for a few weeks, creating as many as twenty-five in a sitting, until it stopped. Then I hung them up and looked at them. It was a new way of getting into my feelings.

Try this process and see what words spark ideas for you.

isn't
nature
remarkable

Bractéu
tilleul
noir

Seed pod to
Parachute (twigs)

landed on my table

Le Haut Meswil

August 10, 1997

Writing It Down
quiets the mind and welcomes our feelings

Every project in my life originates with writing in a notebook or journal. I like the portable format, because it allows me to capture ideas in the moment when I'm out and about. Don't think this will necessarily be a straight line. Your thoughts will take many directions, sometimes turning in circles and then coming back to their starting point. Think of this as exploration. This process of paying attention to what you're feeling, your ideas, and who you are becoming by observing your thoughts and habits will lead you to recognize what's most important to you.

For my new life and my new home, I wrote endless lists, ideas, thoughts, and feelings. They became a script. The dialogues and descriptions were in-depth and clear. These feelings and ideas moved, changed, went away, and were replaced by clearer and more specific thinking and feeling.

Having figured out the **What,** the **How** will take care of itself

come fly with me

fill the air with outrageousness

Les Cottages
Chester (Environs) MI.Lake Douglas. Saugatuck

JB
Aug 25.02
Barn

Furniture
to Keep:—
Jim table
Jim Buffet
All living Yes.
room
~ furniture
library.
barn
— Yes.
beds? New
tables,
— Lower

Description—the cottage is a
safe, nurturing place
quiet and within reach of
a small, charming village.

The cottage is white light bright
while also being enveloping—
fun + playful, cozy.

The cottage is my home and
my playrooms + playstations
There are many nooks
of every kind of place

... station is in the
lower level and is accessible
... to the other — Materials
... a way available
... every activity is to

... play stations interact
... everyday activities
... meals, a bar, a buffet
... hanging out
... with friends —

Expecting
"the
unexpected
Cottage"
dream

27

Writing Your "Housing History"
offers clues to your next kingdom

Writing your housing history is like a treasure hunt. What you find are memories of how you've lived, reminders of those things you still love and those you're happy never to experience again. Write your housing history, as I have here, and then highlight the highlights. I wrote my housing history first and later created the mind map on page 30, and I was amazed to see what I found when I went back and compared the two.

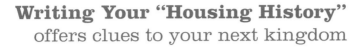

The first house I remember was a **small**, two-story, wood frame house in Kalamazoo, Michigan. There **wasn't much grass**, but it had a **front porch** that I loved. We could **easily walk** to the corner store, which featured a gumball machine. **Convenience** counted even then.

Later, we lived in the **country** with a small lake in the backyard and a bigger lake across the street (after all, we were in the land of lakes). A golf course ran along our road. This was a ranch-style house my parents had **built**. I can still remember the **cozy family room** and the "formal" living room with the grand piano. My own room had **tons of sun** and a private bath. I loved that room and its **generous bed** for girl-friend **sleepovers**.

Many years—and many houses—later (post-college), I wound up in New York City. It took having three roommates to be able to afford the Upper East Side furnished apartment. This **one-bedroom** apartment resembled my tent at Girl

28

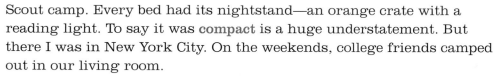

Scout camp. Every bed had its nightstand—an orange crate with a reading light. To say it was **compact** is a huge understatement. But there I was in New York City. On the weekends, college friends camped out in our living room.

Subsequently, I've lived in a weekend home at the beach, a **converted** hay barn in the woods, a beautifully **restored** sixteenth-century manor house, and apartments in Europe. And now, here I am in a 1924 **cottage** in a **charming** corner of New England.

In all of these places, starting with Girl Scout camp—the tent with the minimal cot and nightstand—I had a **vision** of how I wanted things arranged around me. My obsession for **making a space mine** even migrates to hotel rooms! In my years of traveling solo, I carried candles, watercolors, favorite books, and journals. Upon arrival, I always checked the room— and still do—before moving in. If the room didn't fit but my budget couldn't do better, I'd try to negotiate **more light, a better view, a higher floor, a quieter corridor,** or some redeeming quality that would make my stay more pleasant.

Creating a Mind Map
a different kind of list

As the brain moves around, it doesn't naturally list things in a logical fashion. Ideas flow in random order. This is a free-for-all opportunity. Of all possible creative tools, mind maps are the best for capturing fleeting brainstorming moments and eventually organizing your thoughts in an organic sort of way. Made popular by Tony Buzan, the mind map captures the ideas off the center theme you're thinking about. It allows for ideas to tumble out without worrying about sequence or hierarchy. Start using this technique with clues from your housing history. Buzan's book, *How to Mind Map®*, offers a myriad of versions on the theme. Once learned, mind maps can become a positive habit.

Asking Ourselves the Big Picture Questions
finding your rightful spot

Here's your chance to speak up and let the Universe know exactly what you long for. Asking and answering the "big" questions with honesty will help you recognize your needs and wants for life.

Saying you don't know is sometimes more about being afraid to say what you want. Don't feel as if you have to share these writings with anyone else (not yet); these are your private musings about your new space, which don't require the opinions, criticisms, and unsolicited advice of others.

Big Picture Questions

What do you . . .

want

need

feel you must have

think you would love to have

know you absolutely can't live without?

Write. **Rewrite.** Cross off the things that are no longer true. The clearer the picture of **what you want,** the more likely you **will find it.**

My Big Picture Answers

I want . . .
not to feel alone
to be near neighbors of all ages
to see my neighbors
to feel safe
to feel free
a home I can easily manage
one floor living–with space for guests
to walk to a village
to be able to ride a bike to the cafe

I need . . .
a design space
a small yard
to be able to step out on the
ground and dig in the dirt

My new space must have . . .
a campfire circle
charm possibilities
a solid framework
quirkiness
some design detail but
not a design wonder

A crazy roommate motivated me to move. My home has to be a place I can walk into and immediately feel relaxed and happy to be there. I was desperate to find something livable and inexpensive. When I came across my apartment, I fell in love with it! My very own bathroom was my must-have. And my bedroom is my favorite room because I can be alone when I want to be.

MARCELLE, 21
STUDENT
SEATTLE, WA

Who Am I?
becoming authentic
in our personal expression

I think of transformation not as a goal but rather as a process. It's probably not a conscious effort but more an organic following of one's heart and intuition with messages that come to us. When we have the desire to change, to do things in more authentic ways, it becomes an exercise in listening to our Inner Voice and making the internal changes that move us to our authenticity.

Transformation has no time-table, ticking clock, or time sheet. It's one of those things that unfolds gradually. At some point in time, we look back and know that things have changed, and, as a result, we are transformed. We're invited to begin our process when we choose to do so. The conscious journey will be worth the effort and eventually will be cause for celebration.

Emotionally wounded or newly launched into the World— they can feel the same.

34

Divorcing and needing to leave my "in-disrepair" home of thirty-one years caused me to buy some acreage and begin plans for building my new home. By listening to my heart, having lived in a space that was problematic for too long, I just keep asking myself, what do I want and need? I have started a book with things torn out of magazines. I want character, uniqueness, energy, smart, low-maintenance, and a Southwest earthy style. I have drawn up some plans . . . have talked to some builders, am considering being my own general contractor.

ANNIE, 53
RANCH MANAGER
RIO VERDE, AZ

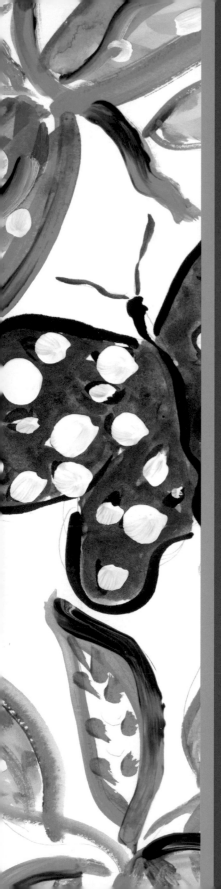

being perfect
is
perfectly boring

A BUTTERFLY ABOUT TO EMERGE

There was no question about it; life had changed and was on its way to more of the same. I envisioned my options, said out loud what I wanted, made and edited the lists over and over again, and created my mind maps. The word "cottage" kept resonating in my head. Cozy, nurturing, healing, nest, intimate, simple, personal became my mantra and my guide.

When I met my soon-to-be cottage, it was Easter weekend. My real estate agent, Lyn, and I pulled up to find the entire family outside washing cars, playing, and riding bikes, waiting to greet us. Immediately, I saw the raw materials to create my imagined cottage. It would become the cocoon for transformation into one of the future butterflies I now see hovering over the butterfly bushes.

Carrot, more like a dog than a cat, came to the car to extend his hello. He continues to do so for all arriving guests. This is a great example of how when you know *what* you want, the *how* will take care of itself.

Having lost my cat to the coyotes while living in my previous home, I told friends over and over again, "I'll get a new cat when I get a new house," in answer to the query, "when are you going to get a new cat?"

It was love at first sight. Did I fall in love with the cottage or Carrot? Both.

Carrot would be at risk in the woods where the sellers were moving, and I showed up needing a cozy cottage and a cat. The Universe is so generous when we get out of Her way and let Her be.

Visualizing
the possibilities
. . . seeing
the picture
and putting
yourself in it.

- What do you see for yourself?

- What do you know about yourself and how you want to live?

- What do you think you need (not what others think you need)?

- What would you like to have?

- What do you want your home to feel like?

- Knowing what you don't want is one step closer to knowing what you do want.

- So, what do you want?

- What don't you want?

- Who and What are in your picture?

Focus Your Vision
and get the picture

Jack Canfield writes about visualizing in his book *The Success Principles™: How to Get from Where You Are to Where You Want to Be.* Principle #11 is "See What You Want, Get What You See." Canfield offers exercises for visualizing your goals—seeing them, "working" them, and manifesting them. The clearer the picture, the more fully you will realize your dreams. I really like the quote he includes from Albert Einstein: "Imagination is everything. It is the preview of life's coming attractions."

Seventeen years ago, my brother died in a car accident. Overnight, my life-view changed. I needed to take stock of my life, and what ensued was a divorce. I left with my young daughter and moved to a less-than-desirable neighborhood. I worked two jobs to make ends meet. At night, after putting my daughter to bed, I would work on what came to be called my dream notebook. I love magazines! So, every night, I tore out pictures that looked like the life I really wanted . . . a caring husband, more children, wonderful travel vacations, a home on the water, and most of all . . . love all around me. Just recently, I found this notebook with the pages torn, the Scotch tape yellowed, and much to my surprise, I discovered all of my dreams had come true, every one of them!

PATRICE, 46
ARTIST
CHESTER, CT

No Architectural Wonder
it had soul waiting to be discovered

Over and over, I've heard women say, "I just fell in love with it. There was this one thing that made it the right choice for me." The one thing for me was, in fact, many things: it was my vision. Admittedly, I had said in advance that I'd be willing to do work on whatever I found. Maybe not this much work. . . .

A house, like a new man in your life, will have issues—things you didn't expect and might not have thought to ask for differently. However, here you are already in love. So get over it and get on with accepting or changing it. (In the man scenario, I don't recommend trying to change him.)

A Design Opportunity
or a design disaster!

My vision did not include 1970's vinyl siding. Somebody fell for the "never have to paint again" sales pitch. This may be true, but it covered up what few architectural details the house had. It covered the rafter tails, the natural warmth of wood shingles, and added the completely crazy shutters that don't even match this style house (even if they were hung on hinges, they weren't to scale with the windows). I don't know who came up with this bizarre idea to add fake shutters.

My vision did not include overgrown trees that hid my favorite room: the porch. Nor were electrical lines on my preferred list—lines that crisscrossed the street and were so weighted down they were sure to collapse one day. Their lack of visual aesthetic was just one more opportunity for improvement. So, underground they went. The gas tank at the back door was not particularly my vision either; it, too, rests underground. So far, I'm still in love.

I don't think I ever "loved" a house right away. I think it's because it has someone else's imprint. But I have grown to love my homes and have always created a space I really treasure. My guiding priniciple for my newest home has been "less is more" . . . while seeking comfort in a small package.

SHEBA, 60
SAN JOSE, CA

i'm not a
fixer-upper,
nor do i like
to be flipped.

my vision

is here

. . . somewhere

41

It took seven years to create my new space and I've never been so happy. This intimate, yet modern, glass, chrome, high-rise space is my nest above the city. I made a conscious effort to make a specific, expensive and limited number of purchases. Books, pictures, plantation shutters, and an old-fashioned club chair add warmth to my otherwise contemporary nest. I love to be alone here and to only invite into this protected space those with the right "aura."

MAUREEN, 60+
FASHION ACCESSORIES
DESIGNER
LOS ANGELES, CA

I saw that my pals and designer friends were questioning my choice (you know, friends who look out for your best interest with the new guy or the new anything). But because of my enthusiasm and clear vision they had the grace not to second-guess me.

What I saw was opportunity, and what they offered was the space to have my vision and then help me to realize it—how generous!

Especially in collaborating with professional friends, I needed to hold to my vision. I couldn't be afraid of having a different opinion or of not being liked—you know the road.

The opportunity to go bigger, go up, go out is the designer's dream. My job was to listen, step back, constantly reevaluate, say yes, say no, respect their opinion, respect my own, and modify the vision as it evolved.

The Porch: it's why i bought the cottage

Starting with what I absolutely knew I wanted was easy. The first absolute was to improve the porch; I could not wait "to get to livin' on that porch." When it was built in 1924, this was the front door entrance.

In the original 1924 version, the "front" door led to a path that brought you to the curb and the mailbox. Now that cars are dominant in our world, the parking area for the cars and the nearest door to it became the main entrance. So as not to confuse anyone, we reoriented the porch door toward the side yard, took away the mailbox, and put in a low stone wall.

The Garage Transformed: creating an outbuilding

My next absolute was to renovate the single-car garage into an at-home studio. This initiated a lot of conversation because it was an opportunity to join the two spaces by using the garage as an entry and creating a breezeway/studio connector to the house. We drew plans, paid for them, and in the end nixed them. This was one of my most difficult decisions. It was logical and a very New England thing to do; we live in wintry weather. BUT, it wasn't what I wanted. For me, it changed the character of the cottage. It would have cut off the backyard accessibility and made the breezeway/studio a pass-through, not the private personal space a studio, in my opinion, needs to be. So, instead, I kept the entry where it was and converted the entire garage into my studio.

A Disaster Kitchen: taking time out to consider

The next phase was going to be a whopper. I needed to catch my breath and get my mind around the fact that the kitchen was a disaster. Since I'm not a cook, it felt adequate for the kind of cooking I do (although the aesthetics were definitely missing). I was overwhelmed at the first mention of needing to redo this space. I knew it needed serious help— I simply could not go there at the moment. Here's what I did and what I recommend to anyone doing a major project: Step back, take a deep breath, and just PAUSE.

*taking the time
to watch the world go by*

The Big Pause

Wait for the emotions to settle.
Stay clear
   of what other people
          want for you
    until you want it for yourself.

Don't be in such a hurry to decide
       this,
         that,
          all of it.

Let the decisions sit on the to-do list
     undecided.

Watch as the choices become clear
      naturally,
     organically,
 quietly.

Making an **–ing** List
what's happen-ing where

Somewhere early on, I made a list of all the activities I saw happening in this cottage. I call this the "-ing list." This really great exercise allows you to plan in advance (while expecting things to evolve) what you want to do where and how the available spaces may lend themselves. If you're moving walls or creating new areas, sooner is better than later.

We can get carried away thinking that every activity needs its own room. But, in fact, many different things can happen in the same place when you have planned for it. Bigger is not necessarily better—it's a sure way to kill intimacy.

-ing activities	room/area
art making	studio, storage
hanging out (summer)	porch
prepping food	kitchen
cozying up (winter)	living room with fireplace
sitting down for meals	dining room, porch, fireside
sleeping	one bedroom with large bed
hosting guests	not necessarily traditional bedroom
guest bathing	need a second guest bath
exercising	meditation/yoga room
parking	under the cherry tree
sewing	dining table
packing	sitting area in bedroom
reading	most anywhere
watching TV	I don't
dancing	I dance through the house

Tables and Rooms
how many rooms do you really need?

For my space, I'm more interested in how many tables are available than how many rooms there are. I've lived in large homes, and I know that every room is not used to its max. With enough tables in the appropriate rooms, projects will find their way to the table best sited and suited to it. Review your –ing activities. Review your available tables and fill in the blanks.

For me, each project has a different nature and needs a different mood and setup. I find I don't mix up the writing projects with the watercolor or collage projects. Some projects are strictly for the office/studio and never come home, such as product design projects that require collaboration and reference materials that live there, not here.

‹ The dining table is best for an overview of a project.

⌄ The wicker porch table is the best "all-around" table. This is more about where it's located. I love the breezes for writing and eating almost every meal, alone or with friends.

‹ The living room side table next to the comfy chair is the wintertime version of the porch table but with a fireplace.

The outdoor painting studio has three tables dedicated to painting, and the downstairs studio (pictured below) has the same dedicated to collage work.

The one room I would encourage in every home is an arts and crafts room, studio, workshop, or separate office. A room that's dedicated to your favorite –ing activities and doesn't have to be picked up and put away will welcome and encourage more spontaneous creativity.

• • •

No one can do it alone—or has to for that matter. You will need help creating a new space, even if it's just for moving in, so get ready for how to ask for help and get it. . . .

you mean i don't
have to have
all the answers?

WHO TO ASK

This is a skill worth developing—

asking for help. Some of us think we're less than perfect if we have to ask others for help. It's good to remember that asking someone to help is one of the highest forms of compliment. Most of us love to be asked—it's our opportunity to give back.

The Cast of Available Characters

Whether you're moving into an apartment, building a new house, renovating, or reorganizing your life, there are lots of people out there just waiting to help.

Someone who's done what you want to do • A very talented friend with time on his/her hands • A good and trusted friend • Someone with a good Rolodex; a database will do • Real estate agent • Financial person • Interior designer • Contractor • Handyman • Architect • Banker • Tradespeople—plumber, carpenter, heat and air company

take pity on yourself—
it's a pity party

I wouldn't know **who to ask** even if I did want help.

I wouldn't dare to ask a friend—she'll see how **vulnerable** I am.

I don't know how to find great **help.**

I'm **clueless** when it comes to finances.

My partner was so much better at this.

Where is he now?

Being **alone** is really the pits.

I'll just spend lots of money and it will be **terrible.**

I have no imagination at all.

I don't know how.

I'm not an artist.

Only creative people can do this.

I don't know how to decorate or to make good choices.

My house is so dinky, **why bother?**

On and on it goes . . .

so, what's the point?

I am not this, I am not that, I am no good at, and I'll never, ever. . . .
Well, so far we're good at whining, complaining, kvetching,
pretending, blaming, sinking, and drowning. We're not creative,
certainly friendless, unimaginative, and generally helpless.
What else is left?

I AM
declaring for myself

Every "I Am" statement is a declaration to ourselves and to the Universe about who we are and what we believe about ourselves. They're also statements of what we are choosing for ourselves. Declaring our "sad and pathetic" self to our subconscious, it (our subconscious) indiscriminately hands it back and gives us exactly what we've asked for. This is a huge ouch! The subconscious does not distinguish, discern, or analyze what we say about ourselves. It simply responds and gives back the experience of what we are saying. In times of crisis, we're at risk of experiencing moments of insecurity and a lack of self-confidence.

Creating a new space or home is already nerve-wracking and tension producing. HOWEVER, here we are with an opportunity. Just try the following affirmations. Even if you can't get yourself to fully believe them or imagine knowing more than you give yourself credit for, try these. "I am becoming an expert in real estate" or "I am welcoming all this new knowledge" or "I am trusting my choices" or "I am willing and excited to ask for what I need." Make up your own affirmations, each beginning with the most important: "I am."

The Knack of Following the Trail

When you're in the market for help, you can see it as a game. Each lead, each name or name of a service, leads to the next lead. The game is to ASK. You will literally build on the answers to the questions with more questions. Each time you meet someone and get help, he or she will answer questions *and* invoke more questions yet to be answered, and on and on it goes. See yourself as getting educated whether you're renting, buying, sharing, or even house-sitting.

i am woman hear me!

We painted the same five walls five different times and each time stood back and said, "nope, that's not it." I learned through our last project that by hiring a designer you can pay her to unify your thoughts (and colors) and listen to your frustrations—a designer can play many roles. And they're not just for millionaires!

SACHA, 52
WRITER, LIFE COACH
EAST HADDAM, CT

54

The Wife of the Painter: Joan and Jim
buy an air-conditioner and get a painter . . .
talk to everyone

Keep in mind I'd never met Joan. It's a hot, rainy, horrible June. I'm buying an air-conditioner and I say to Joan:
"Do you have a unit that fits into the wall?"
"Yes, but if you have vinyl siding it isn't possible."
"Well, I have vinyl siding for the moment, but not for long."
"That's good," she says.
"Why's that?"
"My husband is a painter, and you can't paint vinyl."

Imagine that. I need a painter, and fast.

"Oh, does he have any spare time? I want to move into my new house with the interior painting completed and the clock is ticking.
I guess he's working outside."

"Well, he's trying to, but there's no sun in sight."

Not shy, I ask, "Can we call him, now?!"

"Here, you talk to him. Jill, Jim.
        Jim, Jill."

"You'll be at my house at eight
        tomorrow morning?
        Great!"

By noon
Jim is on the job
and color
is appearing.

Steve the Architect: from idea to paper

An architect needs to draw up concepts and plans (other than on a paper napkin) in order to pass renovations through a zoning board (as in my case) or to obtain certain permits. Professional drawings will prevent (hopefully) major mistakes or misunderstandings. For better estimating and budgeting purposes, it helps to have plans. Steve brought the entry and kitchen concept to life and designed it to connect with the existing framework. One of his great ideas was the trim line that wraps the entire building and visually anchors the building to the site.

Karen: design from the heart or don't design

Collaborating with a talented interior designer and friend is both an amazing opportunity and potentially difficult. We both love these projects and have strong opinions. I knew I was working with a cottage concept and had done a lot of thinking about this in creating the vision, which made it easier to say Yes or No as Karen suggested ideas. Saying No was not always easy—it often isn't. But I learned to accept that No was just getting us closer to Yes.

You can imagine the questions here:

- No, I don't want to go bigger.
- No, I don't want to blow out the living room and add a bedroom.
- No, I don't want a bigger bathroom.
- No, I don't want to create a different staircase to upstairs.
- Yes, I need lots of help with the kitchen. All I know is that I don't want overhead cupboards.
- Yes, I love the oversized moldings.
- Yes, Yes, Yes to the cottage shelves that house my objects and unite the rooms with this perfect solution.
- Yes, the idea to use complimentary colors top and bottom is brilliant.
- Yes, color on paper is not the same as color on the walls. Yes, I need help. No, it does not hurt my ego, even though I'm an artist and I'm supposed to know about color.

My best investment was hiring a decorator. She not only helped me with the decor of the house, she also helped with the building decisions. Her experience eliminated many bad decisions, wasted money, and headaches.

MARTHA, 54
TEACHER
STATESVILLE, NC

55

This is really a pain . . . but before I hire any builder or handyman, I completely price out the job myself. I get the costs for the sheetrock down to the nails, then add extra for labor and a fair profit. This way I have a worksheet from which to evaluate estimates and as a way of thoroughly thinking out the project before starting.

DAYA, 50
YOGA TEACHER
DEEP RIVER, CT

The Design Process
the power of pictures

This is when you pull out your notebook, your lists, and your magazine tear sheets and present them to those who are about to help you realize your vision. This is a great reminder moment for you as well. The more time you spend with your Big Picture, the clearer it becomes.

Having a concept, and a Big Picture, is what will keep your project on track. Having your design concept (a cottage in my case) will make decisions so much easier. If a color, material, scale, or texture choice responds or resonates to your idea of a villa, a ranch, or a Japanese pagoda, then your choices and design decisions will become obvious to you.

Here's an example: Modern, sleek, chrome light fixtures don't exactly resonate with a Japanese pagoda or a cottage. You get the idea. A good designer will edit and show you a limited number of choices. If you're the one doing the shopping, keep in mind that you do not have to see *all* the choices. You will make yourself crazy. A good designer or professional will eliminate the awful, the ugly, and the hideous choices and only present the ideas that correspond to your stated vision, both in design and in line with your budget.

Money, Budgets, and Planning
make the experience more enjoyable

Figuring out the finances is such a personal process. The subject of money is not always easy. But it is essential to discuss the specifics of the various budgets. You absolutely need to consider the timing of expenditures and allocation of funds—even the procurement of funds.

Cosmetic only

Painter + materials

Furnishings

Yard + Garden + materials

---

design

Architect
Interior Designer
> designer
> installer

Landscape

Real Estate

Initial $ Investment

Fees — sometimes negotiable

Closing Costs

Budget Categories

Time line — SCHEDULE

---

financing 'get creative'

net from a Sale

$ needed

Bridge loans

Mortgage

Equity line

Contractor or are you it

Define the scope of work

Estimates get 2-3 WHAT'S NOT included?

PACKAGE Budget

PHASES - budget

SUB - contractors who + what

Builder

ESTIMATES:
SCOPE of WORK
FIXED $?
Time + materials?
Budget CAP?

Handy man

DIY do it yourself

Value $ your time

hire what can't or don't want to do

materials

trade services?

SET ASIDE a CONTINGENCY FUND for extras

Do Your Due Diligence
a garbage pit or a tool kit

Especially when under duress, take the
time to interview and select the people
who are going to help you . . . not make
more craziness for you!

Keep in mind that these people are not
your shrink or best friend . . . maybe
later. They'll need to know certain details
of your life, but not all the dirty laundry.

No matter who you're about to work
with, get references. Go see their projects.
Let them explain their approach to their work.
See what they're proud of, notice what they're apologetic
about, and ask yourself why they are apologizing or
complaining that such and such didn't work out as

no more –
you do not need one more person in your life who is abusive, disrespectful, and not 100 percent on your side

hoped. This apologizing and complaining could be masking a lapse on their side. Blaming the client could be a tip-off about their inability to respond to the needs of the person who hired them. That could become you. Pay attention!

Take a look at their truck or their car—is it a garbage pit or a tool kit? Take note.

Next up is an offering of ideas in this room-by-room tour of the cottage. . . .

more than a roof
over my head

sharing ideas

ROOM BY ROOM

The secret to using every room

lies in setting up the room exactly, I repeat *exactly,* as you want it. When you're in the room, you will know if it works. If you discover that you don't want to be there, find out why not. Before moving things around, stand in the room and ask yourself: What is this room about? Who is it? What part of me wants to spend time here, and at what time of the day? What activities and experiences want to occur here? How will it function when I have guests?

Think about how it could be cozier, more functional, or more fun. When you come to know the answers to the questions, you may want to move the furniture or add the one or two things that will make the difference. If the room still isn't functioning, consider reinventing its use. How does it want to be different? Renaming a space triggers ideas. It will start to "act" differently—you'll see.

61

the rooms

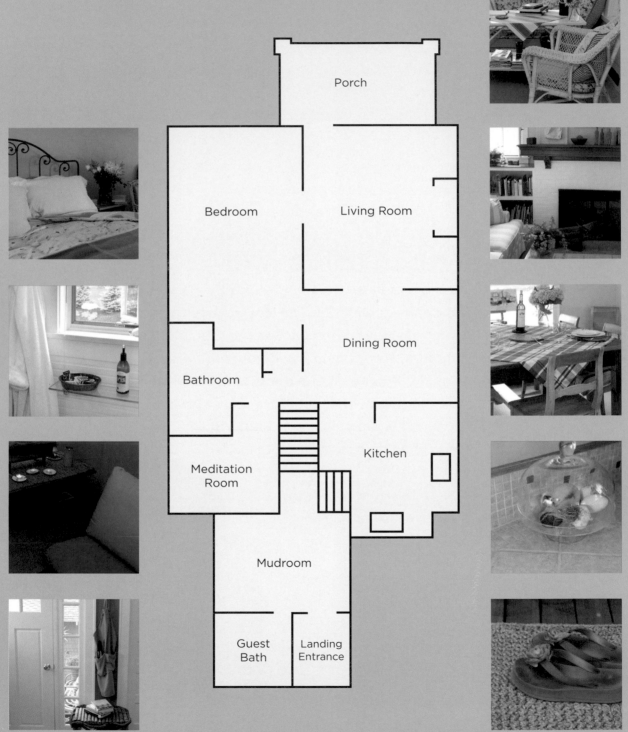

Porch

Bedroom

Living Room

Dining Room

Bathroom

Kitchen

Meditation Room

Mudroom

Guest Bath

Landing Entrance

the landing

The cottage needed a landing, a proper entrance and welcoming area. I waited, looked around, drove about a lot looking at houses, and bingo! This small entry added onto this giant house sparked the idea for the now new entrance. Imagine how little it takes to get an idea once you know what you need. As my friend Sacha reminds me often, once you've identified the "what," the "how" will show up in ways you could never have imagined.

this >
equals this ∨

63

The new landing features a blackboard with chalk that awaits visitors who wish to leave a message or draw a cartoon. My all-time favorite handmade iron bench from France rests here and welcomes seasonal flower changes, the groceries, and packages as they arrive. Neighbors passing by look to see what's new in this ever-changing space.

The "What" and the "How" of the Mudroom

Originally upon entering the house, you were in harm's way of the basement (when the door was open) and the immediate four steps leading up to the kitchen. "Enter at your own risk" was the (un)welcoming message. Adding the mudroom entry was a chance to fill in the blanks of the house.

I wanted it to feel, and it needed to be:

airy
a big, tall "hello" in 200 square feet

cozy warm and earthy

lighthearted
filled with fun stuff

open a welcoming welcome

generous
a gallery for large artwork

inviting
filled with fresh flowers
from the garden

fun artful and practical

curious
an access for Carrot (who, in fact,
refuses to use his personal door)

functional
able to include a full guest bathroom

practical a space for casual coats,
boots, and storage for the vacuum
and cleaning supplies

color
reference
numbers
page 147

mudroom

door & bench

pillow textile

the cozy kitchen

Four steps up and you're in the kitchen. Kitchen design is a specialty—and it's not mine. The only thing I knew for sure was that I wanted to remove the cupboards and add windows to welcome the southern light. Selecting ambient and efficient lighting was crucial. The bistro lighting is reminiscent of Paris and creates a natural and familiar feeling for this gathering place.

I may not cook much, but I do love to draw food. . . .

The bump-out addition of only two feet of space changed everything. In the end it was worth the mess and the stress. We were able to fit a dishwasher (there wasn't one before) and a gas stove with a built-in down-draft (not an overhead). The cottage-style drawers generously hold the frequently used utensils. Why settle for only one style when there are so many possibilities? For the drawer pulls and cupboards, I chose some of each from the available series.

flexible

efficient

my Kitchen

fun

warm

yummy

welcoming

light

bright

cozy

i only cook by color

Granite counters are not the only cool choice. My designer, Karen, introduced me to lots of ideas, including soapstone, fabulous Formicas, and the one-inch porcelain square tiles we settled on. We ran them up the wall and sprinkled them with glass tiles that are playful and unexpected (another Karen idea). They're also heat resistant, strong and efficient, and created the warmth I was seeking. We also used the same tiles to aesthetically join the guest bathroom and retiled the master bathroom floor with the leftovers.

Cottages have an amazingly efficient floor plan (see page 62). They have no long hallways to travel or lost space. All of the rooms spill one into the next. I've discovered that this tight floor plan makes it effective and cozy.

kitchen walls

kitchen trim

tile counter

From the heart of the house, traffic flows naturally. I think it takes about six steps (okay, maybe a few more) to get from one room to another.

■ **Color plays its role** as the connector from one room to the next. Karen and I toyed with my preferred blue and green color palette for the "public" rooms. She suggested that since the cottage shelves already broke the line on the wall, we should use two different shades of the same color—one above the shelf line and one below. It's so subtle, above and below, that at times you can't see it, depending on the light. For the other rooms, we chose colors that felt appropriate to the room and continued with the two different shades above and below the shelf line. Color makes me happy.

molding

green
above shelf

shelf

green
below shelf

blue
above shelf

shelf

blue
below shelf

I wanted a place that was unique to the artist in me. I wanted color, color, color! I experimented with non-traditional room arrangements. My kitchen with its milk-painted bright salmon walls and antique flower paintings and fabrics has a sitting room within it—totally girly. Women love it—men sweat in it!

JUDY, 49
INTERIOR DESIGNER, ARTIST
SHERBORN, MA

roman shades

wood floor

the dining room

Most dining rooms are not used for dining. What's their real purpose?

office

project zone

paint studio

sewing room

snack bar

display area

dead zone

pass-through area

or the guilt room—because we never fix a real meal!

Relax, it can be what you want it to be and can change when you want it to change. My rule, if there is a rule, is that a project can stay out as long as it's a legitimate ongoing work in process. When it sits too long and becomes a storage station or procrastination area (the acid test is if you look at it, you feel guilty), it's time to clean it up. Sometimes just the process of cleaning up inspires having friends in for a meal. So, it's back to being the dining room.

the "lived-in" living room

Is it made for living or for show? A living room likes to be lived in. It needs to work for alone time and for groups—in this case, small groups. Just how small is small? It's amazing how people like to be cozy together, so don't be afraid to over-invite. We'll sit, stand, rub elbows, and be all the happier for the geniality of it all.

I remember living in Paris and having a house-warming party in my not small but minuscule apartment (granted it overlooked Notre-Dame). The French being formal, I spread an elegant tablecloth on the floor and invited everyone to sit for a picnic *à la ameriçaine*.

They were either charmed or horrified and

chalked it up to "oh, those Americans, what do they know about dining?" I did have the good sense to consult *mes amies* about the menu and, most important, the wine.

I've come to appreciate this room as the winter room. The recently installed gas fireplace sets the tone early in the morning and creates instant coziness in the evening. As a Girl Scout purist, I could never imagine resorting to a gas fireplace, but given the lack of hearth or space for wood storage (not to mention having to haul it in), gas became an unexpected solution.

In the summertime this room seems to function as more of a pass-through to the porch, which is the preferred destination.

I am in the process of moving and creating space as we speak. I remarried and we needed a home that was not his/not mine, but ours. The ideas for our new home came from browsing many magazines and going to resorts and experiencing how they can make you feel so relaxed the minute you enter. I wanted this house to be casual, but stylish. I want people to come and feel comfortable, as though they are on vacation; to feel like they can put their feet up and relax; listen to a variety of music; and eat great healthy food, of course, with a chaser of Napa Valley wine.

CYD, 60
MERCHANDISE MANAGER
NAPA, CA

This was the last art piece to find its place.
I tried it everywhere—on the mantle,
                    in the kitchen,
            on the porch ledge,
                              in the bedroom,
and finally here with a stool to support it.
It's the focal point of the room, and it says,

"let's have fun!"

It stops the eye from going all the way
through to the porch while letting it be
known that there's more beyond the
living room.

the porch

we harmonize

It's **the room** that made me buy the house. It was potentially the best room of the cottage. I knew it could be cozy and the breezes would pass through, encouraging naps, not to mention cocktails and intimate meals. It reminds me of camp, with rain on the roof and me safe in my sleeping bag. And, yes, I sleep here often. I love the night noises and the Good Morning sun coming in from the east. By good fortune, the porch faces an empty lot that welcomes Bambi, wild turkeys, and probably coyotes.

*Breakfast, early mornings, afternoon nap, wine and cheese,
dinner for two, this is where I want to be.*

3.21.05

a cozy spot . . . just right for

four gals in their cocktails

of all the things
i longed for,
it was this . . .

the porch reminds me of camp

rain on the roof

safe in my sleeping bag

the bedroom and master bath

One plus one continues to equal more than two. The bedroom serves not only as a bedroom but also as an open closet and dressing area, a sitting area—which becomes an extension of the living room as well—and a desk for the work I try not to bring home from the office. It is the largest room in this tiny cottage. It wasn't built this way in 1924; it was originally two small bedrooms, one opening to the living room and one to the dining room. Thankfully these two rooms had already been joined to create one large room before I arrived. In the fall I change the duvet to a caramel and white pattern and remove the summery rag rugs for a more autumnal look, an easy change that can make a real difference in the ambience of your room.

The bedroom once had a door that opened into the master bath, but I chose to close it up in order to accommodate a built-in counter, vanity, and medicine cabinet in the bathroom on the other side of the wall.

before

bedroom
above shelf

bedroom
below shelf

textile
summer

textile
fall

bathroom
walls

the sanctuary within the sanctuary

This room was initially destined for the TV. I migrated through several options until my mind settled on its current designated use. TV or meditation? Once yoga came into my life it became clear; meditation and yoga won out. I was reluctant to rip out the window and window frame we had boarded up for the new mudroom, so I created an art installation with a collage called "The Woman's Café." A roller shade with a drawing created in Italy was scaled to fit within the window frame behind it. Covering the other window is an interior illustration of La Palette, a favorite cafe located on the Left Bank of Paris, also rendered as a roller shade.

the "guest nest"

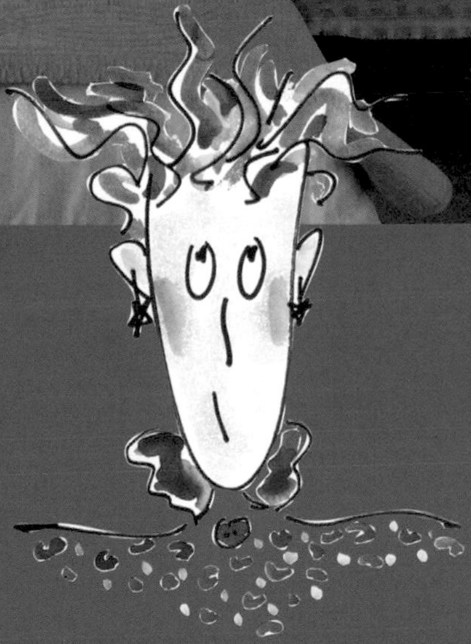

When I asked my brother, "Why do I love this cottage?" he replied, "Oh, that's easy. It's just like Grandma Pearl's house in Lake Odessa, Michigan." I was stunned. I had never put that together, but he sure nailed it! I loved that house as a child. It had a secret upstairs exactly like my own tucked-away "guest nest."

Climb the narrow attic stairs, walk the ridgeline of the roof, avoid a knock on the head, and tuck into one of the two dormers, and you have arrived in the nest for guests. The area sleeps three on a queen bed

i am the bird in the nest

85

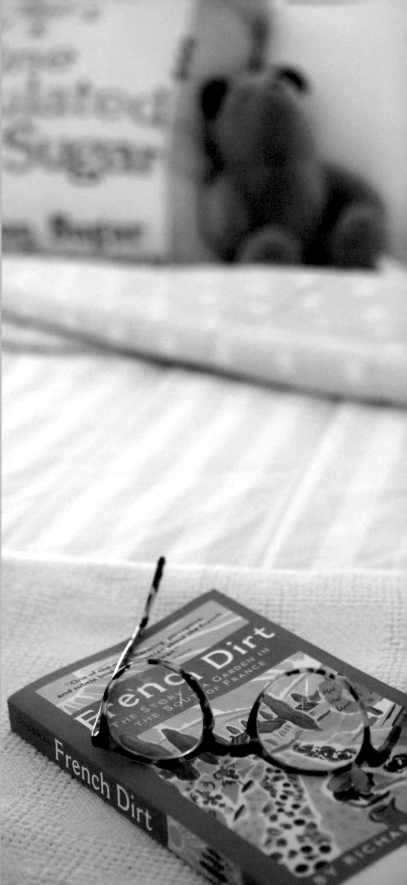

and a sofa piled high with pillows. I lived here for a month in the early stages of painting and renovating the rest of the house. The bed is super comfy, there's air-conditioning, and everyone sleeps well here. There's also more book-shelf space, out-of-season clothes storage, and linen storage.

the guest bath

The guest bath is not hugely convenient for overnight visitors, because it's located downstairs. Since I wasn't of a mind to break through walls and undergo major construction to put in an upstairs bath, we created a full bath off of the mudroom. It has its own heat zone via the towel bar system, making it heat-efficient when not in use. For overnight guests, I make sure to leave on adequate night lights for a midnight descent.

Note how the horizontal bead board creates the illusion of a larger space in this very tall room.

walls

tile

bead board

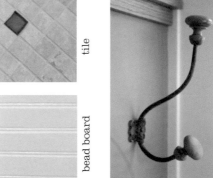

hook

Make sure there is:

good reading light • illuminated night lights in critical spots

an alarm clock and radio

a choice of pillow types

a cuddly friend (if he or she didn't bring one)

fresh flowers

an extra blanket at the foot of the bed and others nearby

a bathrobe with slippers

water on the nightstand • books and magazines (sorry, no TV)

shampoo in the shower

plenty of towels

an extra toothbrush

and considerations to consider

Before your guests' arrival:

are they allergic to your animals

any food dislikes or other, "yikes! can't have that"

what do your guests prefer for un apéritif

red or white wine • porto • mixed drink

breakfast is so specific (it's good to know in advance)

cocoa

what to drink?

coffee tea

milk

sugar or honey

It is daunting to take a less-than-perfect space and decide what improvements will have the most impact. Since this apartment is not our forever home, we don't want to invest a great deal of money in it. However, since we will be here for awhile, I do want it to reflect us and create a space that is satisfying. It is a case of making use of the things that are around us, to paraphrase Raymond Carver. It is important to take the time to make curtains for this home, and not fret over "will they work in the next home." It is about living now, and that is indeed an emotional investment.

MORGAN, 38
EDITOR
BROOKLYN, NY

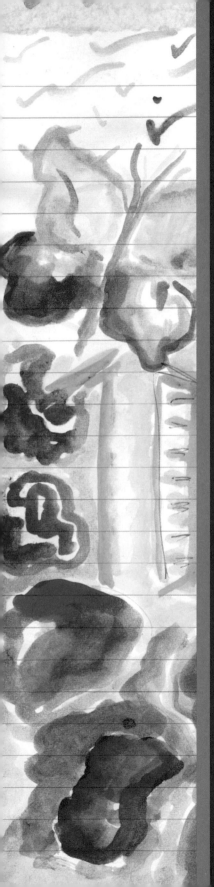

i don't
    decorate
i entertain
        the eye

6

decorate or entertain the eye

GETTING IT TOGETHER ORGANICALLY

I'm not *against* decorating—I'm just not attracted to the more thoroughly planned approach of figuring out what coordinates with what. I guess that means that I arrange things organically as they appear. When I'm faithful to what I like as far as color, style, texture, or feeling, then it somehow comes together intuitively.

If I don't decorate, what is it that I do? I believe that it's the collections in the house that "decorate" it and create an original space. I don't even think of these objects as decorative. They weren't purchased to enhance a corner or show off the mantle, which is what I think of when I hear the word "decorating." Knowing *why* these collections came into my life validates why they live with me.

Objects Tell Their Story

Stuff. What a hopeless word, but nonetheless, it's what makes me feel connected to my life, my friends, and my adventures of being out in the world. The word is more elegant in French and one of my favorites: *les objets*. That at least suggests something artful.

Objects become more than "things" when we take time to consider whether they are what we want around us. These conscious choices take on meaning and value on a personal level. How we feel about them can be profound because of the enormity of the memory they hold. If something shows up in my life that has little or no significance to me, I don't keep it for long—just long enough for meaning to evolve or for me to ask it to leave.

My *objets* have been crafted by a craftsman, created by an artist, wood carver, or ceramist—someone whose hands have intentionally created this bowl, candleholder, or basket. They have resonance. Since I love to buy my artist friends' artwork, I usually choose a small piece so that I can buy more often.

I accumulate stuff.

It's stuff that's needed emotionally or literally.
It's creative to the eye.
It's intentional.
It's a love affair with the
color | shape | material
texture.
It's memory, souvenir.
It's a statement,
a reminder,
a longing
wish or desire
to be | to do
to have.
It's entertaining.
It's silly and makes me laugh.
It's conversational
a moment of exchange.
It's alive.
In the end
it's still stuff.

Training the Aesthetic Eye
learning to see

Having never studied art or taken classes in drawing, I took advantage of my time living in Paris to do something I didn't consciously know I was doing. I came to know what I liked by observing, noting, and making attempts at drawing the things that appealed to me. I'm what is called

94

an experiential learner. I spent time in galleries; I prefer galleries to museums, which instantly exhaust me (must be all those dead artists). Art galleries are alive and in the moment. I bought a postcard, small poster, or catalog of what I found interesting. I watched and observed what attracted me, often sitting in cafes and noticing **everything** around me.

In time, I created a visual vocabulary and a keener sense of how things were designed, how they came together, what I appreciated about them— the feel, color, material, or the unexpected humor of something. When you pay attention to the world around you, you can train the eye and learn to *see*. Resist the urge to pass judgment; instead take the time to closely examine your reactions to what you observe.

 My eye and my longing naturally travel to the crafted piece. I guess it runs in the family, because my father was a pewter smith and my brother a fountain designer. Looking around my small space, I see what I've chosen to keep after my major paring down. I have a personal connection to most items, a story of where I bought the piece, who I was with, and who created it (many of whom I know). Others mark a trip, a *"souvenir de voyage."* When I travel, I like to find something that's indigenous to the area. Often it's a piece of folk art locally crafted. One piece can encapsulate an entire trip, experience, or essence of someone I've met along the way.

 I collect mostly small paintings so that I can display more artwork and afford to have more artists in my collection. This latest addition resting on the shelf to the left was, in fact, a gift. I was given the very first painting created by my twelve-year-old friend, Ariel. I feel honored.

I also gather, I've noticed, objects that represent what I enjoy doing. I love creating art, and these giant scissors represent the cut-paper work I did years ago.

The coffeepots and cups have long represented an attachment to moments in a cafe with a good friend or time spent with the *International Herald Tribune.* For years, I created collages with coffee accoutrements. This piece is entitled "the woman's cafe." As a collage artist, I get to collect art supplies. These materials linger as long as needed until they find their way into a piece.

The postcard rack harkens back to my deep desire—especially while living in France—to create and have published postcards. They so completely epitomize the quintessential travel souvenir to collect and to send. This rack came from a friend who was in the postcard business. For years, I bought racks from her and brought them home to the U.S. and gave them away. I'd bring them in a canvas duffel bag. Oh, the things I carried across the waters! Ultimately, my dream of creating postcards came true, and I worked with a French postcard publisher. Those cards are still found in Paris.

97

Just Enough No spoon lies unused. No bowl doesn't serve or please the eye. There's a fine balance of materials: **Wood** the showstopper ladder **Metal** rusted clock made to run again **Funky kerosene lanterns** I had to have the pair 'cause you always need a buddy **Ceramic** that rattles **Rust iron** stops the door **Glass** blown in Murano— designed by an American woman (pg. 73) **Italian marble Yes Yes Yes**

Basketry created locally **Metal** (from the Australian outback!) crafted the alligator dog **Nature's gifts** exotic pinecones **Iron hooks** found in *une brocante*, an upscale junk shop (pg. 87) **Wrought iron** benches **River stone** a special house-warming gift from the architect **Textiles** art pillows by Karen (pg. 85) **Cashmere** blanket—an outrageous purchase that makes my life feel rich and luxurious!

Shopping choices

Shopping is not a full-time career. If it has become that, get help—unless you're paid well to shop for others, then I take it back! Making good shopping choices is, however, a full-time responsibility. Poor shopping choices generally make us feel bad about ourselves. How many times have we told ourselves we'll lose ten pounds to get into that sale dress? Lose the ten pounds; then see what you really want.

Here's an example of waiting until the right choice comes along. (This process probably applies to a new man as well!) I'm imagining the small lamp I need for the telephone stand that sits between three rooms. I consider asking a friend to build one for me, but it's way too expensive and not really her specialty. Next, I cruise the home catalogs, tearing out many possibilities. I take measurements, because the space is very small and I don't want to knock over a lamp that's too large while racing to the phone. It needs to be stable. Proportionally, the lamp also needs to be short. I'll pay whatever I need to pay within reason. I finally think I've found it, and I order it from a catalog. When it arrives I unpack it and keep the packing materials, just in case. It's fine and solid but not great and in fact takes up way too much

room on this small surface. Back it goes into the packing material, and I take it to the post office. I then find something locally. This one is actually worse. Back it goes; at least I didn't have to ship it.

I let it rest, taking a break in my search for a while. I keep imagining the "just right" lamp. A miracle is about to happen. I see another lamp that appears to meet the criteria. Am I willing to risk another mail-order disaster? I decide I'm up for it, and it finally arrives. This silly lamp does it for me. Now, the lesson is, I didn't settle for what I didn't really want. I was patient. And each time I look at this lamp, I feel good about it and, more important, I feel good about myself. Now, isn't that cool? Oh, and it came with a dimmer, which I hadn't even imagined, and I love that, too.

Got to Have It . . .
filling the emotional hole

We are bombarded daily by 30,000 buying messages and promises: advertising, e-mail, catalogs, TV, radio, magazines, subliminal messages, blatant messages, messages on cars, buses, trucks, billboards, and on and on. Keep in mind that most messages are fear-driven: "If you don't buy this . . . this will happen. If you do buy this, you'll certainly be the greatest and coolest amongst all your friends. You'll be popular. Buying this product guarantees that you'll be happy, rich, sexy. Otherwise, you won't." Says who?

Excuse me, how do *you* know what will make me happy? When the "got to haves" take over, try making something. Recycle things you already have. Reinvent new uses for what you already own. I love doing this— it's so satisfying!

The hole inside is more likely to be filled by you and your creative expression than by buying more stuff that you don't really need. In the end, those purchases can actually make us feel emptier and less enriched.

· · ·

Acquiring. Owning. Enjoying. Our valued stuff demands its rightful place. It's the everyday belongings that challenge the storage problem. Stay tuned. . . .

storage
shows up
in unexpected
places

7

finding places and spaces

Storage. I see it as a game. What's the object to be stored or the category needing a home? That's the first question . . . maybe. Organization often poses one of our greatest challenges. How do we keep it simple, accessible, and suitable to our overall space? There's a sort of game we can play here that requires thinking outside the box.

The approach to storage issues usually follows this pattern: Here are the items to be stored. Where shall I put them? Try reversing the puzzle.

- Here's the answer . . . *what's the question?*
- Here is a shelf . . . *what wants to live here?*
- Here is the mantle . . . *what's the opportunity?*
- Here is a stairwell . . . *how can it be used?*
- Here is an empty basket . . . *what can it hold?*
- Here is a wooden cigar box

    . . . **now holding espresso spoons.**

This kind of reverse thinking often sparks unique solutions. Items normally stuffed into closets could become a more integrated part of the house. Thinking of your everyday things being "exposed" might encourage different choices, knowing you may want, or even need, them to be visible, not tucked away.

Creative Storage Spaces

What do I need where to make my world work more efficiently? In space planning, this is called the adjacencies, which means placing objects near one another for usage reasons and easy accessibility.

Ask yourself, "What do I see around me that can serve to store and simultaneously display a category of things?" Example: this cupboard in the dining room. It's a fixed piece, it's not moving, and it's next to the dining room table. The answer seems obvious. Put the dishes and serving platters here and most of the glassware. Keep a few everyday glasses in the kitchen. Put the bar here as well, limited as it may be. The "better non-silver silverware" has its own drawer here at the end of the table.

The most important investment I made in the house was the enlargement of the kitchen. I added more storage, more room to work, and room for a table. I love being in my home.

CYNTHIA, 64
HAPPILY RETIRED
SCIENCE TEACHER
KALAMAZOO, MI

Question: What can I create to accommodate coats close to the back door?

Answer: Cottage cupboards, featuring primed, but not painted, bead board that looks worn and more *cottage*. The tops serve as a storage-display area, a view especially appreciated from the kitchen level.

Carrot is not a storage problem but rather a coming and going, in and out, problem. We created a cat door by cutting away half of two drawers of this antique pine dresser. Who could know that the official greeter of the cottage would demand a door person and had no intention of ever using this clever cat-door solution? So, I just answer the door a lot. The now slightly deformed dresser (I actually like it this way), accommodates the guest towels, bathroom supplies, and beach towels—not a total loss. Hidden behind the birdhouse collage below entitled "things are never quite what they seem" lies his cat door. This at least solved the display problem of the collage.

My must-have for my new space was more storage. Unfortunately I could not find many places with adequate storage, so I created my own without compromising my living area.

PATRICIA, 60+
DEVELOPMENT COORDINATOR
HARTSDALE, NY

What my mom doesn't tell you are some of her great ideas. She's incredibly inventive—she bought two unfinished wood upper kitchen cabinet units and added a simple custom-built wood top. She didn't get interior shelves or hardware but simply rested the cabinets on the floor along the wall. It was just the right height to work as a ten-foot serving sidebar in the living room. This beautiful piece is now a focal point and looks like a multi-thousand-dollar custom built-in.

MAUREEN (DAUGHTER)

I love walls of books. I love the library at the bottom of the hill. But I have no available wall space! So, where to store the books? The answer: Every category of books lives in its rightful and useful place. My three cookbooks live in a drawer in the kitchen. In the at-home studio reside art books that inspire in the moment; usually these feature living artists' work that interests me. In the living room, you will find the art classics: the mega art books of Chagall, Kandinsky, Klee, Jasper Johns, Christo, Diebenkorn, and more. The garden books migrate between here and the porch, where the current morning pages journal rests along with magazines and a sketchbook. The meditation room holds the inspirational material, and the bedside houses reading of the moment.

kitchen storage

Kitchen storage is probably more about the things we don't use than those we do. Make a list of what you use most often. Having easy access to these items simplifies life. It's surprising how few things we actually use—or is that just me, the non-cook? With no overhead cupboards, I had to have generous drawers. I tend to shop like the Europeans and don't stock up much. I buy fresh often and not usually for more than two days at a time. The under-the-counter pantry drawers have the minimum of the most basic of basics. And the pot and pan drawers have the specific pans that I know I cook with most frequently.

For all the rest, the stairs to the basement were left open, and we built shelves that can be accessed from both sides. This serves as the perfect pantry for the backup pots, pans, second coffeemaker, really large platters, paper goods, and so on. Store the wine downstairs in the cool, dry cellar. Don't do what one friend did and put it in the furnace room. Yikes! Put the backup club soda and tonic in the cellar as well. Keep the minimum of mixers in the kitchen beside the fridge.

it's a puzzle to fill every nook and

Why have a toaster and a toaster oven? The toaster oven with a cutting board slides under the stand that sits next to the refrigerator. The coffeepot just next to the toaster oven rests in a square tray that pulls out for filling the water container and easily tucks back in. The tray also houses the coffee filters, a sugar bowl, plus a collection of antique spoons. Finding the answers to these storage questions can be fun once you decide what you need. Solutions show up. I promise.

Where to put the table linens? I chose to dedicate an entire drawer to this category. I love textiles and use fabric napkins and placemats on a daily basis. I agree, it's a luxury, but I like adding playful color and design to the table. Yummy textiles create a fun table. I prefer organizing the party, setting the table, and graciously accepting food-prep help from friends or the nearest *traiteur* (gourmet takeout).

cranny efficiently and creatively

Bed linens presented a challenge. I did not have an extra closet for them. It took a while, looking around and trying on the options. Finally . . . it became clear. The wall along the stairwell up to the guest nest had a cavity of space behind it. We punched it out and created generous shelves for comforters and the rest—another problem solved. Whew!

storing bathroom products

Towel bar heaters may sound decadent, but they're often found in Europe for warming the towels in winter or drying them in humid weather. They are actually both decadent and practical. There's nothing worse than a mildewed summer towel! Given that cottage bathrooms are cozy (i.e., small), the towel bar heater also comfortably heats the room.

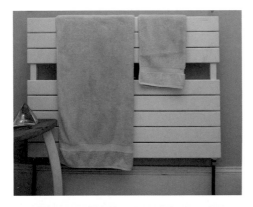

Medicine cabinets are not particularly efficient in a small space, either protruding into the room making it even smaller, or too small to be useful. My idea was to close up one door from the bedroom (who needs three doors in a bedroom?), and in that doorway create a vanity, bath towel, and bathroom supply cupboard. Along the inside wall, a series of narrow shelves were built to serve as an open and easy vanity. Voila!

clothes storage in the bedroom

The bedroom closet bifolds had to go. We threw them out, left the opening, and built the shelves and dresser into the layout. Over the top shelf another well-hidden shelf houses out-of-season clothes and shoes in large, clear Rubbermaid storage bins. Long and heavy hanging clothes get stored upstairs in a space created under the roof.

Clear boxes with clear covers allow for seeing what's inside. Forget cardboard boxes; they're a pain. If you find these crystalline clear boxes out in the world, let me know, because these are the best of the best for storing all kinds of materials—shoes, art supplies, and kid stuff. And I've lost my source.

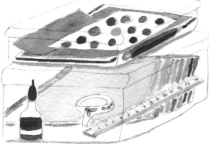

Once our systems are in place,

life runs more smoothly. We don't waste time and energy looking for things and can relax in our user-friendly spaces. It's like our emotional state. Once we're calm on the inside, it's easier to go out into the world. I feel this way about my house. Knowing the inside is settled, I'm really happy to get outside and *play in the garden.*

in
my garden
i
plant ideas

planting ideas

Being an artist does not alleviate the stress of choosing house colors. For the exterior of the cottage and the studio, I wanted a green—this much I knew for sure. I wanted the color to be both unexpected and balanced at the same time. Having vacillated long enough, I called Karen to ask her opinion about which of my three green choices to use. Her reply was, "use all three." But of course!

The neighbors kept a curious eye on the project and continually asked when I was going to settle on the exterior color; they too thought it would only be *one* color. They wondered and watched paint sample after paint sample come and go. The painter, Jim, wondered as well.

Here are the winners! I finally chose Sherwin Williams Wheat Grass and Clary Sage for the house and Artichoke for the studio. You'll find my color chart on pages 128–9 and the color references and numbers in the resource list on page 147.

planting colors

In the intuitive process, or guesswork, of choosing plants, I felt comfortable with the plant and flower colors I liked and how they could complement the exterior color of the house and studio. I was way outside of my comfort zone, however, when it came to the actual plant materials to choose.

With time, I've come to know my preferred plant and flower types, not only by their color, but also by their habits of needing sun, shade, lots of water, or not much. I read their tickets at the nursery and learn as I go. I'm not shy to ask a neighbor about her choices and annually attend a plant swap. This year, I swapped something I took last year from the swap. Is that cheating?

A massive planting of "Nikko blue" hydrangeas along the front of the cottage seemed appropriate in character and color. Adding a ground cover of dark but friendly green myrtle and its early periwinkle flowers also felt just right.

Lavender serves as a reminder of days in France. I had to try growing it, even in this unfriendly New England growing zone. So far, so good. The color and healing qualities greet me and guests upon arrival.

Roses felt so intimidating. But since I inherited some bushes from the previous owners, and as they appear to be thriving without fuss, I'm encouraged. Karen gifted the studio with two "Dream Weaver" rose bushes in just the right shade of red. They were the perfect housewarming gift and lasting celebration of a successful project.

more than the purrfect color

Carrot is not only the official greeter to the cottage, he also fits the color profile of my preferred cat colors. Carrot is quite happy here in what I'm not sure is a bird bath or a bird "catcher." For the moment, he holds the dominant position under the peonies.

One of my best finds are these amazing waterproof umbrellas designed to protect the peonies from the rain, which turn brown the minute the water hits them. I found them so amusing and practical that I also use them to protect the hydrangeas that face the brutal southern sun.

I said to Karen, "I can't decide which green." Her response, "use all three." Bingo!

house

entrance

studio

I love working and living in the garden. The one thing I wish I'd known when I started making my own home was that I would stay here as long as I have (12 years so far). If I had known I would be here this long, I would have made more major changes sooner and enjoyed them longer.

CLAIRE, 64, PASSIONATE GARDENER, ESSEX, CT

The Icing on the Cake
help from Joe—the landscaper

paths create a sense of adventure

A tasty cake with no frosting is not appealing even if the cake batter is superb. Joe the landscaper and I met for coffee to share ideas on several wintry Sunday mornings. For the street side, I had the following concept: keep it simple, no fortress of trees to the neighbors . . . a visual softening would be nice. For the backyard, again no fortress. Instead, Joe had a terrific idea—to create a berm (raised soil bed) nearly the length of the property, which would visually level the site from its downhill position. We then planted in a friendly way to soften the view toward the next-door neighbor.

To connect this modest one-third-acre property, I took a spray can of paint and painted wiggly, sexy lines in the dirt. What fun! We then mixed stones of various sizes for the appropriate areas. A connected path of different ground materials now wraps the house and studio.

and destination

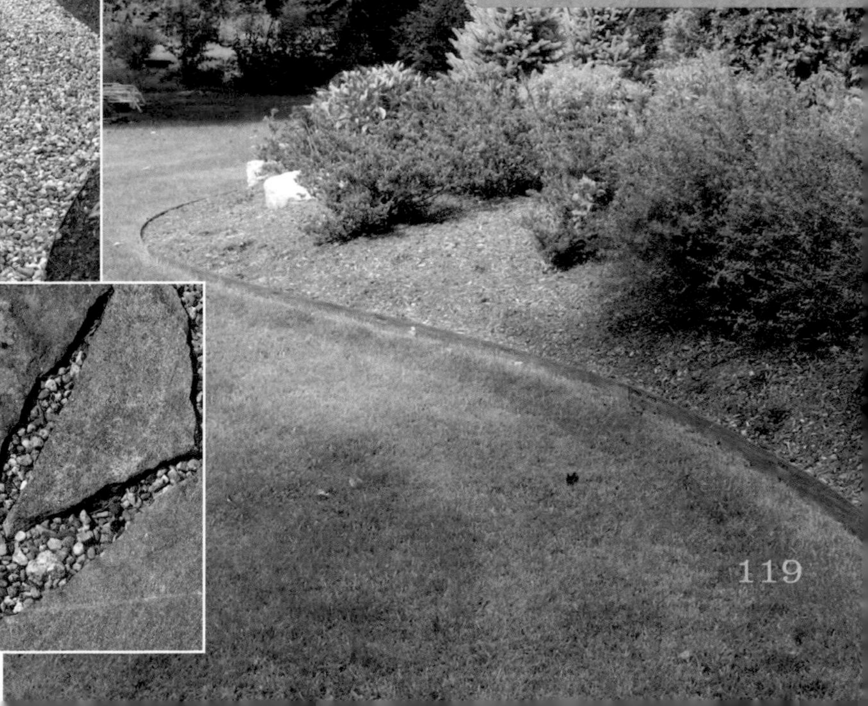

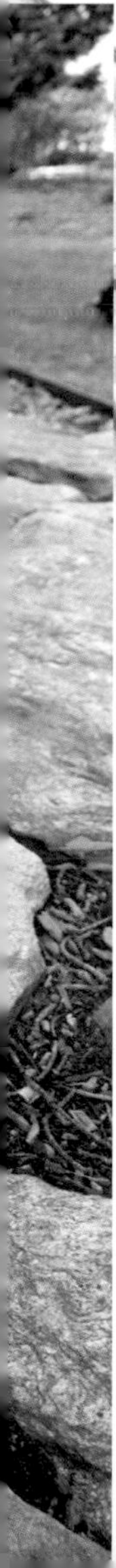

I finally had enough money to purchase a home. I desired a space that was soft in texture, not cluttered, where I can relax and read, or tend to my garden. Having a view of wildlife is very important to me. It's still a work in progress! A garden is what I absolutely had to have.

NANCY, 48
MEDICAL ASSISTANT
GALLOWAY, NJ

The Yard as Collage

As the eye travels around my yard, one finds different vignettes, or short stories, told through found objects, which are mostly worn and rusted.

As a collage artist, I see the yard as a playground for art projects and for opportunities to create installations, a fancy word for put-together stuff that in my mind tells a story. Since I collect a fair amount of *objets trouvé* (translation: quality junk), creating drama in different corners of the yard makes it playful and unexpected. Vignettes sprout up in surprising places.

The tree collage is entitled "the artist's phone booth." Its apron suggests that the artist is off doing other things while time passes.

I'm not a serious shopper unless I'm on a mission, but I love this sign coupled with the beat-up zinc potting table. This table suffers from such severe rot and has been propped up so many times, I fear for its life. But in the meantime it sits under the cherry tree and, while it lasts, it holds the seasonal pots of impatiens that love the shade. Way too soon the mood here will change to pumpkins with fall branches, and eventually to pine boughs and discreet Christmas decorations (no flashing reindeer noses or Santas coming down the chimney!).

The picket fence bench that sits in the middle of the now exuberant yellow coreopsis has become the way station for gardening tools. It suggests that there's always work to be done. Keeping these tools handy nudges me to tend the garden. Hidden somewhere in here are kitchen herbs and a few pepper plants because I love their colors. The crafted birdhouse is a "welcome" to my nest.

I planned for four, maybe five, areas where one can sit and the eye can wander. Off the porch area, there's a stone bench quarried from nearby. A sitting area on the post for the bird often puzzles those in passing. Is it real or not? The best was when I witnessed a wren sitting on top of this permanent fixture and leaving its calling card.

Coming around to the front there's the twig furniture grouping that's being eaten by the squirrels and deer, and serving as a scratching post for Carrot. It's coupled with what reminds me of a Parisian street bench. I like this area because it's slightly hidden from the street by the Kousa Dogwoods but still remains marginally in view for a friend passing by who wants to say hello. I welcome hellos.

even birds need a nice home

If you're a "bird" looking for a nest, we're open for rental by the season or on an annual basis.

I've been gifted with several birdhouses to celebrate my own renovated nest. Each one, when viewed, evokes the giver of the gift, over and over again.

See the garden as a healing tool
    for growth and success.
Forget the plants that keeled over or
    the grass that burned up in the
    boiling southern exposure.
You would, too.
Notice nature's abundant and
    forgiving nature.
Watch the colors unfold
    as the season ripens.
Notice as newness arrives—
      butterflies flitting around
        the butterfly bush.

I needed a yard for my daughter and a place closer to work so we could have an extra hour and a half (former commute time) together each day. I didn't need a showplace. I needed grass. I knew I wanted simplicity for our lives and to work and live in the same community. I had already decorated a house and condo, so what most interested me was having grass under our feet when we played.

SHERRY, 41
SCHOOL LIBRARIAN
SPRING HILL, TN

my outdoor studio

Here it is—the studio that almost became an entryway. I love having an outbuilding that I can go to on this modest property. It creates an illusion of having more land (without the upkeep) and creates the privacy zone a studio needs to be.

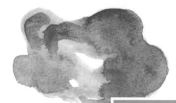

ATELIER

ENTRÉE
DES
ARTISTES

Some mornings, I load up a tray and take breakfast out to enjoy my newly acquired easy chair. The drop cloth "fabric" is a simple covering for a less-than-attractive hand-me-down chair or sofa. The tying of the knots at the corners is what makes it work. I settle in here for writing morning pages and am often inspired to pick up a paintbrush and stay for a while.

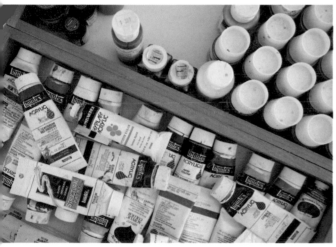

House and Garden Color Chart

a little bit of planning goes a long way . . .
if nothing else, it gives you something
to change.

HOUSE
clary sage

ENTRANCE
wheat grass

STUDIO
artichoke

annuals get
potted annually—
Geraniums with
Lobelia and Impatiens
are favorites

apricot

Salmon + blue

Sweet Peas
garnish the
mailbox

Daisies are
welcome late in
the season

white

A Rose is a rose   is a rose petal

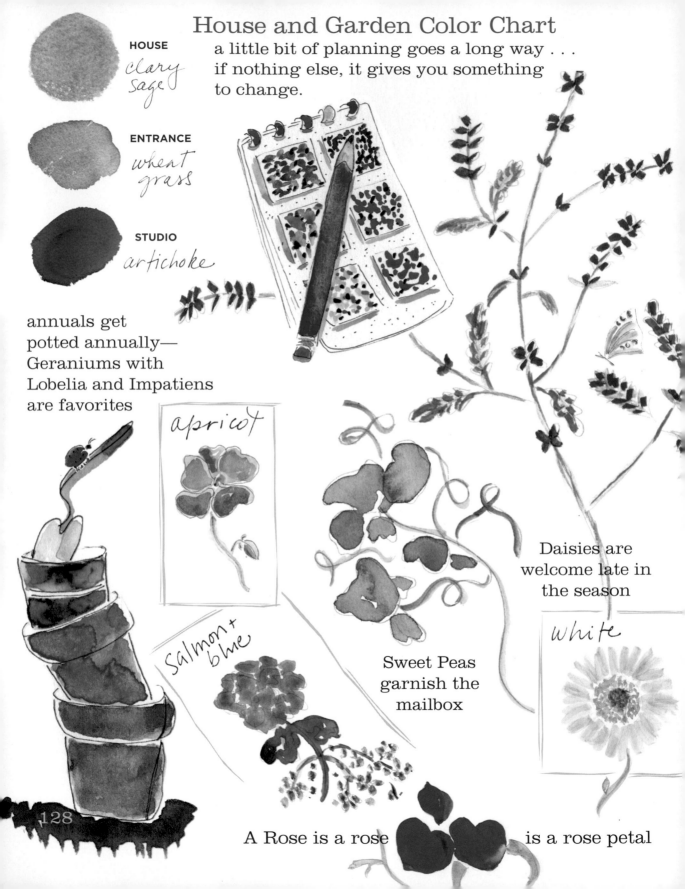

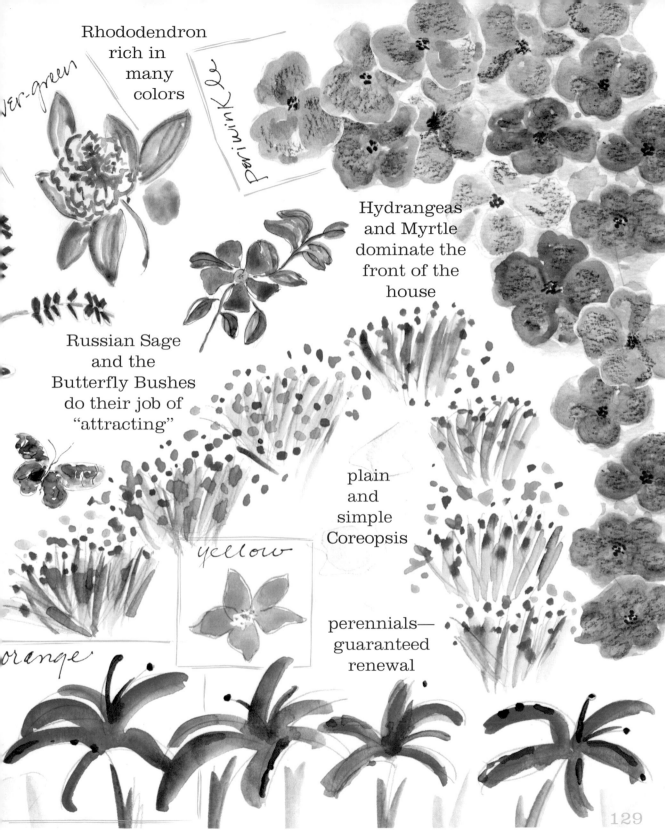

Rhododendron rich in many colors

Ever-green

Periwinkle

Hydrangeas and Myrtle dominate the front of the house

Russian Sage and the Butterfly Bushes do their job of "attracting"

plain and simple Coreopsis

yellow

orange

perennials— guaranteed renewal

129

Day Lilies—say hello along the street

As we know, the season will change and the color palette will darken around this cheery cottage, but we can anticipate magnificent color in the fall foliage and autumn flowers as New England heads into winter.

I may not be a master gardener—how many of us are? But I do know that the mere act of gardening is good for the soul, uplifting like the flowers themselves, and cause for celebration in the never-ending surprises. The garden and the yard also want to be a canvas and a playground for our creativity.

AS ONE JOURNEY ENDS, ANOTHER BEGINS

By the time I finished my cottage, the beginning of a new life had started to sprout. This cottage has been transformed and brought into its next incarnation. It continues to be the placc that cmbraccs mc as I experience my own personal transformation. The butterfly has emerged.

I acquired a butterfly bush with the house and have planted a second. I'd never experienced one before. I'm fascinated to see the butterflies' arrival just as the bushes come to full bloom. They know their season. Nature unfolds. They flit and flutter. They seem to live fully, 100 percent in their darting and gathering. These monarchs also make their journey.

Our nurturing homes are there for us in exactly the right times. Our adventure and story began with getting out the maps, making the reservations, and getting on the road. We did that. We've arrived. But of course, our journey is never complete . . . until it is.

Having come through the divorce and now grieving the death of my brother, York, I am acutely aware of how this cottage wraps its arms around me and allows me to be whoever and whatever I am today. I reflect on these life journeys. They seem to be more transformational than goal-directed. They seem to be about the process that moves us toward our next version of "I am."

Back to the Porch
it's still my favorite

I'm thinking about the recent death of my brother. I can't imagine
how different I might have felt had I not had my nest to nestle in
with the dearest of friends.

Karen called and asked what did I need? How could she support
me? It's exactly these questions that are so hard to answer when we're
numb or haven't yet learned to Ask for What We Need. (Here's that
idea coming around in a different way . . . the remembering to Ask.) I
knew she was about to hang her art show. I knew she hadn't finished
the last painting or finalized the prices. I could relate to all of those
things. And still she persisted: "This is not about what I'm doing, this
is about you." Gently but firmly she prodded: "*Just tell me if you
want me to come over.*" Taking a deep breath, I barely whispered,
"*yes, please come*" and burst into tears.

Karen spent twenty-four hours with me. We sat on the porch while
it poured, listening to the sound of the rain on the roof as we talked
and cried, until we finally got up from the sofa and went to the village for lunch and ice cream. We talked late into the night, shared
coffee in the morning, and then off she went to finish her show.

LEARNING TO LIVE WITH AN INCOMPLETE 'TO DO' LIST

"I'll do something for myself as soon as I complete my 'to do' list . . ."

completing the 'to do' list is not a life goal nor does it give much meaning to one's life.

'to do' lists are essential to everyday management . . they're also an excuse for not getting on with what really matters

the problem with 'to do' lists is that they are <u>never</u> completed

give yourself permission to cross off the things that no longer have meaning

inventing things to put on your 'to do' list is not the best way to use one's creative imagination

simply by making the list . . . some things seem to take care of themselves.

Respecting our efforts, focus, and the work required to create our nests, it's time to take a break, to put away the planning and our "to-doing." It's time to enjoy and to celebrate this journey.

i'm learning to live with
an incomplete "to do" list

this, of course, is easier said than done

"the **to do** list"

i'll do something for myself
as soon as i complete my "to do" list

"to do" lists are essential
to everyday management . . .

they're also an excuse for not getting on with what
really matters

give yourself permission
to cross off the things that no longer have meaning

simply making the list . . .
(some) things seem to take care of themselves

inventing things to put on your "to do" list
is not the best use of one's creative imagination

completing the "to do" list
is not a life goal
nor does it give much meaning to one's life

the real problem with "to do" lists is
they are never completed

Celebrating My Neighbors

campfires—wine, cheese, and marshmallows

I love having neighbors. I love seeing them walk their dogs or their baby, or speed-walking and fast-talking as they buzz past the cottage. Neighbors are community. They are backup for emergencies, there for a hello, a welcome home, or a helping hand. I enjoy seeing their homes in close proximity.

I used to be hidden in the woods; God forbid I saw a neighboring property. Now I'm curious to see what others do with their homes and gardens, how they choose to spend their time playing baseball, washing their car, gardening, or just hanging out. It's all good.

neighbors
fill in the blanks

neighbor is different from friend

neighbors create community
a sense of belonging
a sense of safety

neighbors borrow things
because they know they can

neighbors help carry, move,
and offer opinions

neighbors invite when it's
appropriate, not because
they should

neighbors fill in the blanks
when there's no guy around
to help

neighbors keep you posted
on neighborly news in a
neighborly way

neighbors look after the cat

the neighborhood cats have
their relationships

neighborhood bonfires attract
like fireflies

there is life after change

new opportunities to be experienced

returning to the roots.

doors close

we have to accept that

new doors open

we have to believe that

pause

long enough to notice

realize where you are

look around and see

maybe for the first time

create your world your way

My butterfly house continues to serve as a place to heal, a place from which to review the past and begin to imagine a different future. Yours can do the same. For me, the renovation and transformation became a major focus. It required (and continues to do so) asking over and over and over again: Who am I?

"We shape our dwellings and afterwards our dwellings shape us." —Winston Churchill

notice by the time your project is finished the moles will have arrived, the flowers will have re-emerged, the neighbors will have become friendly and welcoming

celebrate no matter how large or small your new world, space, or place it is monumental and worth celebrating

completing the circle

 Authors Coaches Teachers

Joe Ruben & Monica Landry
life coaching, guide, vocal
www.vocalfit.com

Daya Soudan
Yoga, Integrated Movement
860.526.3109

Jack Canfield Trainings
visualization
www.canfieldtrainings.com

Tony Buzan
mind maps
www.buzanworld.com

Lynne Twist
The Soul of Money
www.thesoulofmoney.com
www.pachamainstitute.com

Julia Cameron
The Artist's Way
www.theartistsway.com
The Official Julia Cameron Web site

 Design, Build and Related Services

Karen Beckwith
Interiors, Color, Art
413.637.4479

Bob Antoniac
General Contractor
RJA Construction
860.434.5152

Steven Frantz
Custom Builder
studio, closet, porch
860.526.2544

Mike McCulley
Commercial Real Estate
860.526.5548

Lyn Hanberg
Residential Real Estate
860.767.2133

Sal Osso
Majestic Electric
860.691.1851

Jim Wrynn & Joan
Painters
203.245.2653

Steve Lloyd
Architect
CT and Vermont
860.526.5094

Joe Cerase
Landscaper
860.399.6695

 Creative Services
they are the book

Lisa Bousquet Photographer
Interiors, weddings & more
www.LisaBousquet.com

Nancy Freeborn
Graphic Design
860.526.5441

Bob VanKeirsbilck
Graphic Design + Illustration
www.longcatgraphics.com

Tim Marth
Crossword puzzler
chantydog@yahoo.com

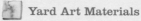

Places
Two Quintessential Southern New England villages

Chester, CT
"The Best Small (Creative) Town in America"
www.visit-chester.com

Essex, CT
"The Best Small Town in America"
www.essexct.com

Color Reference

Sherwin William's for Exterior Colors
www.sherwin-williams.com (for Store Locator)
Door and Bench: Lupine SW 6810 69
Entry: Wheat Grass SW 6408 117
House: Clary Sage SW 6178 117
Studio: Artichoke SW 6179 117

Benjamin Moore for Interior colors
www.BenjaminMoore.com (for Store Locator)
Entry/Mudroom: Kingsport Gray HC 86, pg.69
Kitchen: Lenox Tan HC 44, pg. 72
Dining room: Iced Mint HC 2030-70 (above shelf), pg. 73:
   Hancock Green HC 117, (below)
Living room: Ocean Air HC 212350 (above), pg.73;
   Palladian Blue HC 144, (below)
Porch Ceiling: Lily White 2128-70, pg. 80
Floor: Showroom White
Bedroom: Filtered Sunlight 2154-60, (above), pg. 83;
   Straw 2154-50, (below)
Master Bathroom: Lake Placid 827, pg. 83; Trim: White Blush 0C 86
Meditation room: Standish White HC 32 (above), pg.84; Wilmington Tan HC 34, (below)
Guest Bathroom: Lenox Tan HC 44, pg. 87

The Whites throughout: by Benjamin Moore

All trim: doors +panels, window molding, brackets +shelves: White Opulence semi-gloss OC, 69

Ceilings: White Opulence flat OC, 69

Crown moldings: Mayonnaise gloss OC, 85

Answers to puzzle on page 52.

147

acknowledgments

The group at Globe Pequot Press and now skirt! have published my journeys in France and now this very personal journey that has brought me back to the US. I thank Mary Norris, executive editor and Lara Asher, acquiring editor, both of whom helped to craft my words and shepherd the project along its path. Without their help, you'd be reading a laundry list of ideas, albeit, good ones!

My thanks to graphic designer Nancy Freeborn, who edited hundreds of photos and crafted the book. My continued gratitude to Bob VanKeirsbilck, with whom I've worked for nearly ten years. Thanks Bob for the "icing on the illustrations" and the coziness in the corners. I thank the team behind the scenes at skirt!, some of you I know personally and others I experience and benefit from by your willingness to team play. Additional thanks goes to Susan Braden, Features Editor at *Shore Line Papers,* for her guidance and editorial encouragement.

There's no one who knows the cottage better than I, except Lisa Bousquet, our photographer. She has seen every corner from the lens of her camera and her creative eye that I've so come to appreciate. Lisa's generosity of time, and her willingness to get it right, is what made this project possible and fun! Thank you, Lisa.

Casey, Maeve, and Dan O'Brien had the good sense to sell me their first house (to build their dream) and to give me their cat, Carrot, who needed a home. Thank you all.

148

And to Casey, a special thanks for the "before" pictures. They hugely contributed to the telling of this story.

My ideas are the integration and interpretation of what I've gleaned and personalized from the many sources I so appreciate! There are boundless materials and teachers to learn from. I particularly wish to acknowledge the following:

I thank Julia Cameron for writing *The Artist's Way* and creating the concept of morning pages. Not a day goes by that we don't meet on the page. You must drink a lot of coffee, or something, with all of your followers.

Jack Canfield, of the Chicken Soup series, I remember from days gone by. I was brought back to you through *The Secret* and followed the trail to your book *The Success Principles™, How to Get from Where You Are to Where You Want To Be.* Thank you, Jack.

I was introduced to Tony Buzan's *How to Mind Map®* through Time Management years ago and I haven't stopped drawing them since.

Lynne Twist's book, *The Soul of Money*, came into my life and the why appears so clear. Every time I read your book something major happens that moves me forward along my path. I admire your contribution and dedication to the possibility of better choices for our lives and the world.

Daily I am in deep gratitude for all who are my teachers, knowingly and unknowingly.

I thank you.

No man or woman stands alone.

design draw paint cut glue
write create play
if it's not fun, I'd rather not do it!

NANCY DIONNE

Jill Butler is a self-taught artist, illustrator, designer, and creativity coach. Her designs appear on collections of home furnishing products; her collages are shown in U.S. and European art galleries. Her creativity workshops are a recipe for living.

Jill's most recent creations are the Birds of a Feather now known as JillsBirds'nWords™. The Birds, used throughout this book, speak her voice as well as a universal voice. This flock, both men and women, are now winging their way into collections of giftware, paper goods, gift books, and home-related products.

Jill loves to travel especially when she can move in and set up home, whether it's in a hotel room or another kind of space. Her most extensive move-in was 16 years in Paris which gave birth to three books about France: *Paintbrush in Paris, Rendez-vous with France,* and *Wandering Paris.*

Jill's return to the U.S. created another kind of journey, as chronicled in this book. No matter where she is, she is creating . . . and "no matter where I go, the who I am goes too".

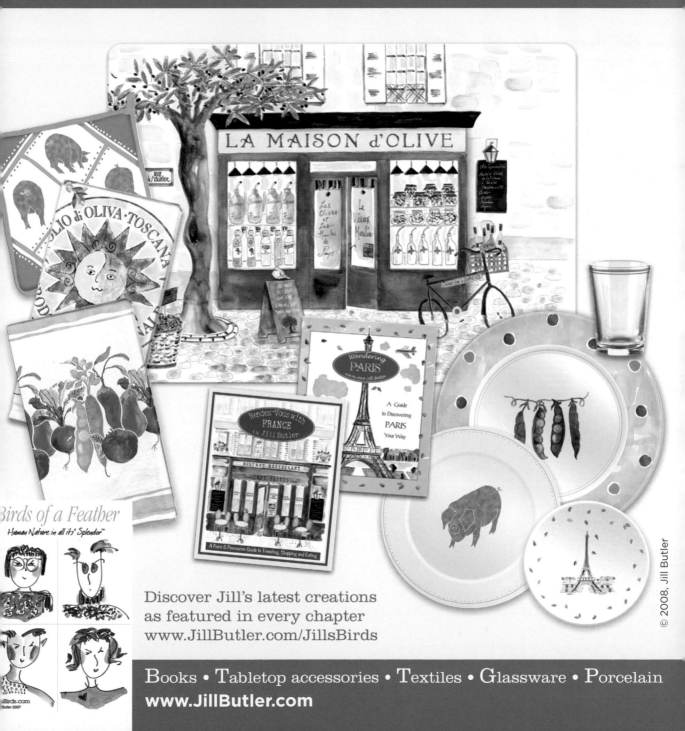

The artistic journey continues with gifts to celebrate the space you've created for yourself.

LA MAISON d'OLIVE

OLIO di OLIVA · TOSCANA

Birds of a Feather
Human Nature in all it's Splendor

Wandering PARIS
A Guide to Discovering PARIS Your Way

Rendez-Vous with FRANCE
by Jill Butler
A Point & Pronounce Guide to Traveling, Shopping and Eating

Discover Jill's latest creations
as featured in every chapter
www.JillButler.com/JillsBirds

© 2008, Jill Butler

Finally, a
skirt!
that fits!

www.skirt.com